FORGOTTEN HOLLYWOOD FORGOTTEN HISTORY

Starring The Great Character Actors
of Hollywood's Golden Age

MANNY PACHECO

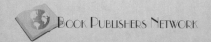
BOOK PUBLISHERS NETWORK

Book Publishers Network
P.O. Box 2256
Bothell • WA • 98041
PH • 425-483-3040
www.bookpublishersnetwork.com

10 9 8 7 6 5 4 3 2 1
Printed in the United States of America

LCCN 2009905931
ISBN10 1-935359-16-9
ISBN13 978-1-935359-16-6

For every book sold $1 will be donated to MOOSEHEART CHILD CITY & SCHOOL.

MOOSEHEART CHILD CITY & SCHOOL is a residential childcare facility, located on a 1,000-acre campus 38 miles west of Chicago. The Child City is a home for children and teens in need, from infancy through high school. Dedicated in July 1913 by the Moose fraternal organization, MOOSEHEART cares for youth whose families are unable, for a wide variety of reasons, to care for them. The Moose fraternity provides children with a wholesome home-like environment and the best possible training and education.

Moose Charities Inc., is a registered nonprofit, Illinois-based 501 (c)3 charity, charged with the primary goal of providing the necessary resources for the continued support and maintenance of the MOOSEHEART Child City & School and the MOOSEHAVEN retirement community. Additional donations can be made to Moose Charities 155 South International Drive, Mooseheart, Illinois 60539-1100. Email inquiries about Moose Charities Inc. can be made at request@moosecharities.org.

Editor: Julie Scandora
Cover Designer: Nina Barnett
Typographer: Stephanie Martindale

This book is dedicated to
Margaret Prouty
(1919-2009)

A creative inspiration in my life. She had a tremendous love of black & white movies and shared this enthusiasm with her children and me throughout her life. Her legacy lives with each printed word in this work. I will miss my beloved grandmother.

Basil Rathbone

Claude Rains

CONTENTS

FOREWORD

GARY LYCAN

THOSE OF US WHO WORK IN THE NEWS and entertainment
industry are fascinated by history. I'm not sure if it is because we are
dreamers caught up in thinking about "what if…", or realists who see
events as they actually happened and want to document it for future
generations, whether it be audio, video, film, or a musical composition, or perhaps a story written online, for print media, magazines, or books. Yes, books, something one still picks up and reads and turns pages, as you are doing now.

I've seen a fair amount of history. I was 21 and working Saturday nights on the wire desk at the Orange County Register. It was past deadline, around midnight. The presses

THE WHITE HOUSE
WASHINGTON

January 27, 1967
7:45 p.m.

Mr. President:

James Webb just reported that the first
Apollo crew was under test at Cape Kennedy
and a fire broke out in their capsule and
all three were killed. He does not know
whether it was the primary or backup
crew, but believes it was the primary
crew of Grissom, White and Chafe.

Jim Jones

Memo to President Johnson
(regarding Apollo 1 fire)

starting to roll, when the wire service (*FLASH -5 words or less*) reported *"Churchill Dies."* It was Jan. 24, 1965, more than two years after I worked an entire weekend when JFK was assassinated, Nov. 22, 1963. The events unfold like chapters in a book for me – *three astronauts die in Apollo fire in 1967, RFK killed in 1968, Elvis dead in 1977.* The one story we layed out pages for and wrote headlines that made us feel jubilant – *man landing on the moon in July, 1969.*

TRIBUTE TO

Senator Robert F. Kennedy

By Senator Edward M. Kennedy

ST. PATRICK'S CATHEDRAL
NEW YORK CITY
JUNE 8, 1968

ON BEHALF OF Mrs. Robert Kennedy, her children and the parents and sisters of Robert Kennedy, I want to express what we feel to those who mourn with us today in this Cathedral and around the world. We loved him as a brother and father and son. From his parents, and from his older brothers and sisters—Joe, Kathleen and Jack—he received inspiration which he passed on to all of us. He gave us strength in time of trouble, wisdom in time of uncertainty, and sharing in time of happiness. He was always by our side.

Love is not an easy feeling to put into words. Nor is loyalty, or trust or joy. But he was all of these. He loved life completely and lived it intensely.

Edward Kennedy Tribute to the late Robert F. Kennedy
(partial text)

Along the way, I started writing a radio column, and later began producing a program about saving adoptable animals called *The Pet Place.* Along the way, I have met many personalities. One is Manny Pacheco, a native of Los Angeles who loves political science and history and probably would be a lawyer today had it not been for a diagnosis of kidney cancer while a junior in college. The prospect of a possible life cut short made him change direction and decide to be an entertainer. Luckily, the diagnosis was incorrect – his kidney merely had an abnormal shape. He changed majors and went on to become a successful radio personality in L.A. on several different stations. For Manny, "history" spun off into a unique knowledge of the oldies radio format.

But Manny's fascination with political science never waned. If anything, it kept nagging at him as he saw people relying more and more on internet reading, and "history" that is either colored by ideology, poorly written, or just plain incorrect. The result is this book – "*Forgotten Hollywood, Forgotten History*." It was an admittedly risky undertaking, profiling a selected group of Hollywood character actors and connecting their choices of film roles to the actual history or folklore of the persons they portrayed. One can easily walk a tightrope when writing a book that appeals to both fans of old Hollywood and those who love to read about history.

"That's one small step for a man, one giant leap for mankind."

Apollo 11 Moon Landing
Commemorative Postcard

Overall, Manny does a skillful balancing act. This is one of those books you don't want to read in a rush. Allow yourself the luxury of a chapter at a time, embrace the storytelling method that merges fact and fiction and delivers some fascinating insights into some of cinema's favorite character actors. So, go get the popcorn, sit back and relax, and let the show begin…….

Gary Lycan,
Radio columnist, Orange County Register;
Executive producer and co-host, Pet Place television show;
Public relations director, VPI Entertainment

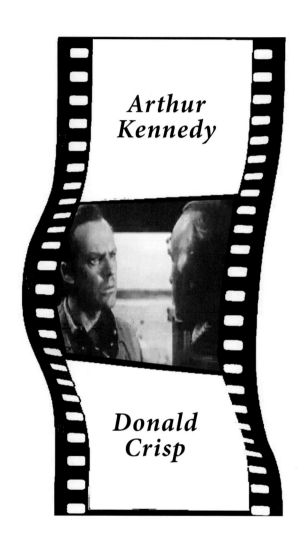

*Arthur
Kennedy*

*Donald
Crisp*

PREFACE

APART FROM VISITING YOUR LOCAL LIBRARY, or looking through Wikipedia in today's computer age, it has become increasingly harder to come in contact with American history. As a member of the baby-boom age, I grew up going to school that required history as part of a full educational curriculum. The Golden Age of Hollywood and the early days of television were filled with projects from noted novel-ists and playwrights in dramatic reenactments that brought to life a time that existed before I was born (which was 1957). The source of original films and teleplays of the period might have come from Charles Dickens, Rudyard Kipling, Jules Verne, Mark Twain, John Steinbeck, Edna Ferber, Sinclair Lewis, Eugene O'Neill, Ernest Hemmingway, Dashiell Hammett,

Writer Paddy Chayefsky

Tennessee Williams, Arthur Miller, and other great authors of the nineteenth and twentieth centuries. Rod Serling, Abby Mann, Paddy Chayefsky, and other noted script and screenwriters were not afraid to be controversial and intelligent in approaching thought-provoking issues of the day.

President John Adams *(portrait)*

While watching the adaptation of David McCullough's Pulitzer Prize-winning book, *John Adams*, brought to life recently on HBO, I realized that this kind of television programming is disappearing from American society. After deep soul-searching and plenty of channel surfing, the only place today that I can find any significant references to our precious U.S. History is on PBS, C-Span3 History, Turner Classic Movies, and, of course, the History Channel. Snippets may also be shown on the Discovery Channel, the National Geographic Channel, A&E, and ESPN Classics. Otherwise, reality TV permeates network and cable television.

Every once in a while, Hollywood provides compelling cinema that may be historical in nature. Usually one can find these gems around award season. Then they go away and hibernate for the summer, to be replaced by inferior sequels and remakes, mindless horror movies, crass comedies, and weepy "chick flicks."

The computer is a valuable tool in finding educational and informational facts. The problem is that catalogues are too broad and non-categorized, and the temptation for today's youth is to search for what is popular in our society. Gaudy styles of the week have replaced the significant substance of the past. I also fear that the slashing of funding of the National Endowment for the Arts and Humanities by the government might further erode the memories of our rich presentation of history.

Before it becomes completely extinct, I decided to write a book that ties Hollywood's past reverence of American history to how the U.S. actually evolved, linking events that occurred during our pre-Revolutionary days to issues that we might tackle in the new millennium. That said, it would have been easy to pick familiar stars of the thirties and forties. Much has been written about Clark Gable, Gary Cooper, Spencer Tracy, James Stewart, Bette Davis, Katharine Hepburn, James Cagney, Cary Grant, Henry Fonda, Ingrid Bergman, and John Wayne. I decided instead to challenge the writer and reader by selecting character actors; the supporting players that help define generations of history. Each has had a unique career by tackling different periods and issues with regards to our great republic.

Looking back on our history, Wyatt Earp has little to do with Senator Everett Dirksen; Charles Lindbergh with Helen Keller; Horace Greeley with Alvin York; Babe Ruth with Ayn Rand; P. T. Barnum with General Douglas MacArthur; or perhaps President Chester A. Arthur with Jackie Robinson; except all are part of this book. They are part of Americana, rich in its diversity and interesting in the tales passed on through the generations. Award-winning novels also play a role in our cherished past, for they manage to capture the imagination of a people, not with celluloid or video but with rich textual characterizations from the power of the pen.

The character actors I have selected may not be remembered much now, but that is the point. They shouldn't be forgotten. Additionally, for those bit players that I have not included in this book, that does not necessarily diminish their importance in the presentation

Charles Coburn/Gentleman Prefer Blondes (trailer)

of our U.S. history. Frank Morgan, Charles Coburn, Jack Carson, Peter Lorre, Dean Jagger, Alan Hale Sr., Sydney Greenstreet, James Gleason, Lee J. Cobb, Ray Walston, and others were fine supporting players with interesting stories to tell.

David McCullough, Ken Burns, and Robert Osborne are devoted to the American experience. They are true inspirations to us all. I dedicate my efforts to them. This project is an experiment of interest to me and, hopefully, to those willing to read something a little different. I find that writing my first book has been enlightening and truly creative in the best sense. I had to write it...and I'm glad I did.

Frank Morgan/Great Ziegfeld *(trailer)*

Jack Carson/The Hard Way *(trailer)*

ACKNOWLEDGMENTS

I'D LIKE TO ACKNOWLEDGE those special individuals who made this effort possible. Without their contributions, this book would never have been written…

Laurie Pacheco – My wife always believes in all endeavors I approach. Her unconditional love and support is immeasurable. Like the credit card commercial says: *She is priceless*!

Manuel and Gloria Pacheco – I have been doubly blessed that my parents have been by my side through all my accomplishments in the area of entertainment and creativity. They always believe I can succeed.

Virginia Vandewouwer – My sister becomes closer to me each day that I live, and she has become one of my best friends. Her husband, *Roland*, has been a strong and faithful ally to her, and I thank him for that.

Matthew Vandewouwer – I personally want to thank my nephew for his photo editing expertise that helped this book come alive. He approached this project with true professionalism.

Peter Parker – My close friend has shared a love for movies and history with me for a decade. Our appreciation for the past has made these actors stay alive in our souls. I bring our passion to this book.

To the many friends I have that supported this project including **Candice Worl**, **Russ Duke**, **Sam Ayers**, **Jade** and **Skye Wheeler**, and others that have shown interest in the subject matter. They kept me motivated throughout these past months of work.

I'd also like to thank the folks that I met along the way that were generous enough to help me. These individuals are no longer strangers. They include: **Ivan Smith** of Canning, Nova Scotia; **Heather Moore**, photo historian, U. S. Senate Historical Office; **Rutha Beamon**, National Archives and Records Administration; **Amy Elizabeth Burton**, Curatorial Assistant, U. S. Senate Commission on Art; **Steve Zeleny**, Director of Archives and Data Management, International Church of the Foursquare Gospel; and the directors and staffs of the various presidential libraries that allowed me use of photographs including the Franklin D. Roosevelt, John F. Kennedy, Lyndon B. Johnson, Richard M. Nixon, and Ronald Reagan Libraries.

I'd finally like to offer my appreciation to **Sheryn Hara** and her staff at Book Publishers Network. She has guided me on every step of this journey from writing to publication and, I'm sure beyond, into distribution. I am convinced that Sheryn is a rare breed that is truly committed toward the accomplishments we search for. She is dedicated to the author in us all, and this makes her quite special!

INTRODUCTION

THE LINEAR HISTORY OF THE UNITED STATES has been well documented over the years. It's taught in schools, and our national conscience moves in a forward-thinking direction. We look at our past, and we say it began with the arrival of the *Mayflower*. Then the arrow points and stops at moments of reference until we reach the present.

U.S. Flag Presented to Founding Fathers *(portrait)*

An actor in Hollywood moves from project to project until the time has come to retire. Motion picture themes are based on the interest or availability of the source. Also, auditioning and casting is part of the process. What's fascinating is the sense of purpose that emerges from analyzing an actor's work. We can see that by type-casting, or through intentional choices, the development of a career with some meaning.

The subjects in this book were enormously busy during Holly-wood's studio era. Only by looking back can we really understand how fruitful they were in tying their work with a thread of commonality. In other words, these individuals in good faith delivered an overall consistent message fashioned from the body of their performances and, in some cases, their private lives.

This book doesn't present history in any specific time frame. Rather, it's a patchwork or quilt of differing eras, based on the scope of the actor's career. Each chapter unfolds in the general order the films were produced. I offer analysis on the chosen subject matter of the motion pictures, and/or the inventive motivation of the author's material.

The book's compelling feature is the overall differences of style and substance of my fifteen subjects; as contrary as the design of the United States and its rich past. This is the historical perspective that makes my project individually unique. Here are their stories…

CHAPTER ONE

THE LOYAL OPPOSITION
Claude Rains (1889-1967)

CLAUDE RAINS WAS AN ENGLISH-BORN ACTOR that painted his film career around questionable historical figures and sophisticated scoundrels of varying degrees. He appeared in movies that transcend American history, from its pre-Revolutionary spirit through the Allied fight against fascism and into the Cold War. In between, he was cast with one of his favorite co-stars, Bette Davis (her memoirs reveal a reciprocal admiration), in drawing room dramas, "weepers," that offered a respite from his constant look to the past. His range in acting helped him break his early typecast in horror movies (*The Invisible Man* made him a star). A valuable suggestion by noted director Michael Curtiz challenged Rains to underplay a scene, much as Spencer Tracy did in most of his movies. To his credit, Rains developed a persona that made his great movie villains more memorable. Movie audiences would watch Rains, and they accepted his rich characterizations. His nomination four times for Best Supporting Actor underscores his gift.

Adventures Of Robin Hood
(trailer)

His first important foray into history captures him playing the son of Henry II of England. As Prince John in *The Adventures of Robin Hood*, Rains creates a nobleman whose lust for power and wealth would cause an uprising from his subjects. John would be eventually banished from his aspiration to the throne. In truth, he was the brother of Richard I (the Lion-Hearted), a king in the tradition of Hannibal, Alexander the Great, Julius Caesar, and his own father. Richard had a great hand in the expansion of the British Empire in the twelfth century with campaigns in France, Sicily, and Palestine. However, these wars did little for his subjects. When Richard died on his way back from a stop in Vienna, John moved from his brother's shadow. He created the Magna Carta, considered the cornerstone of English liberties. His allegiance in maintaining Norman land in France became his undoing with regards to his reputation.

Richard The Lion Hearted
(drawing)

Magna Charta

Actually, British attention to lands accumulated throughout history at the expense of its people was the country's ultimate downfall as an empire. For example, taxation of the American Colonies of various goods and services, such as stamps and tea, without due representation in English Parliament led to unrest, our Declaration of Independence, Revolutionary War, and the subsequent creation of the United States of America.

Napolean III

Execution of Emperor Maximilian I *(photo)*

In *Juarez*, Rains is cast as Napoleon III. He is the evil French monarch that places Maximilian I as the puppet ruler of Mexico at a time when revolution was ripe in the fledgling country. A small film role, Napoleon sets the stage for the heroic struggle of the Mexican indigents led by Benito Juarez. What makes this story more tragic is the supposed benevolence of Maximilian over a people that neither understood nor liked the emperor. Maximilian's execution in the wake of insurrection underscores the inspired backlash towards an unforgiving despot back in France.

As Sir John Talbot, Claude Rains returns to the horror film genre in *The Wolf Man*. Obviously knighted and presumably loyal to the crown, he seems to understand little about the American education of his son, played by Lon Chaney Jr., or the European superstitions surrounding a lycanthrope (a man that changes into a wolf by a curse). The pathos of the movie comes from the victimization of the title character, played by Chaney. Mentioned throughout the film: "Even a man who is pure in heart and says his prayers at night may become a wolf when

Tammany Hall *(circa 1915)*

JAMES A. GARFIELD
REPUBLICAN CANDIDATE FOR PRESIDENT

CHESTER A. ARTHUR
REPUBLICAN CANDIDATE FOR VICE PRESIDENT

Garfield/Arthur Campaign Poster

the wolf bane blooms and the autumn moon is full and bright." Eventually, Sir John (the name an obvious homage to the earlier character that Rains plays in *Robin Hood*) comes to terms with his son's mystic affliction, and his tragic confrontation with the werewolf legacy.

In 1939, Claude Rains became a citizen of the United States. In honor of this accomplishment, he took on a role of complex proportion in **Mr. Smith Goes to Washington**. In Senator Joseph Harrison Paine, we see a conflicted character that is noble by title but compromised by the spoils of power and lobby groups. Political machines grew in the Industrial Age of America in the late nineteenth century. Graft and political favors were among the gifts provided by unscrupulous politicos of the period. New York's Tammany Hall was particularly ripe for corruption and patronage, beginning with William M. "Boss" Tweed and, later, Senator Roscoe Conkling. Both political parties were guilty of these practices and this led to great upheaval, particularly during the elections of the era's presidents. In fact, Rutherford B. Hayes was selected, not by a popular vote (for which he was in the minority) or by electoral vote (which he technically lost). Rather, he was chosen in a closed-door committee, which tainted his one-term presidency. A disgruntled office-seeker, who favored political machines, assassinated our next president, James A. Garfield. His successor, Chester A. Arthur (a protégé of the New York Stalwart political dynasty) put a temporary end to such practices with the signing of The Pendleton Civil Service Reform Act of 1883. Appropriately, Senator Paine in *Mr. Smith* finds his soul and comes to the aid of his filibustering colleague in the Senate (the James Stewart character) accused unjustly of graft.

The early forties was a turbulent time for the U.S. The country was committed to neutrality that would keep our troops out of a another World War. Yet, President Franklin Roosevelt felt compelled to help Europe and, notably, England from the Nazi threat.

It was in this atmosphere that ***Casablanca*** was written. Rains plays suave but corrupt Captain Renault, the Prefect of Police in the French territory in Morocco. The Vichy in the North African deserts were French sympathizers to the German campaigns that were commanded by Field Marshal Erwin Rommel, a decorated military man. (Rommel seems to have had no implicit knowledge of Nazi atrocities that were going on through much of Europe at the time.) The Humphrey Bogart character, Rick Blaine, is a cynical bar owner; scorned in love, but not without a history of fighting for revolutionaries in Spain and Ethiopia against the encroachment of fascism. It is Rains that steals the movie by playing both sides of World War II for his own political expediency. An early statement by Capt. Renault frames the man: "I have no convictions ... I blow with the wind, and the

Field Marshal Erwin Rommel

Casablanca *(trailer)*

Claude Rains (1889-1967) ❧ 5

Casablanca Conference (1943)

prevailing wind happens to be from Vichy..." His closing down of Rick's bar because of gambling after collecting his roulette winnings is particularly amusing. But, his utterance of a most memorable line (in a movie of memorable lines), substantiates the problems Germany would have in obtaining loyalty from the French, who truly desired to be rid of Hitler's agression. After a Nazi officer is killed by Rick, Capt. Renault asks his subordinates to "round up the usual suspects" to protect his friend and brother in patriotism. This is a powerful message to Americans new to the fight from the unprovoked attack on Pearl Harbor months before. It also didn't hurt the popularity of the film that President Roosevelt and British Prime Minister Winston Churchill held a summit in Casablanca during the early part of our involvement in World War II.

Claude Rains was also adept at subtle comedy. In **Here Comes Mr. Jordan**, he plays an angel that inadvertently takes the soul of a man that is not destined to die for decades. His diligence in rectifying this wrong is heartwarming. The film is a pre-cursor to **A Guy Named Joe** and **It's a Wonderful Life**. The fantasy genre is uniquely American in movies made during the period.

In **Now Voyager** and **Mr. Skeffington**, Rains tugs at the heart-strings of audiences that appreciated his subtle nuances and approach to melodrama. Even broad pathos could be attained by Rains, as captured in celluloid in **The Phantom of the Opera.** Application of his craft would come close to perfection in his next major role...

Notorious ties the fight against Nazis with the impending Cold War. The master of suspense, Alfred Hitchcock, was the right director for this film project. His choice for screen vil-

Claude Rains/Now Voyager (trailer)

lain: Claude Rains. As Alex Sebastian, Rains proves to be at times menacing and not without pity. One suspects that his love for the Ingrid Bergman character was sincere. It is entirely plausible the beautiful Bergman could fall for this suave spy. At the same time, she loathed what he stood for. His undoing is swift and cold, as he faces certain death at the hands of his cohorts against freedom. It is a masterful display of fear and cowardice, with a hint of dignity, that only Rains could muster. Though he did not win the Best Supporting award for his performance, many thought he was the favorite, until the selection of Harold Russell from **The Best Years of Our Lives.** The "atomic age" and the era of McCarthyism has its roots in this Hitchcock classic.

Claude Rains was popular on television in the fifties. He appeared on **Alfred Hitchcock Presents** a number of times. He also co-starred in the celebrated **Pied Piper of Hamelin** with Van Johnson. Rains is the mayor of the hamlet that hires the minstrel to rid the town of rats. When he refuses to "pay the piper," the children of Hamelin are sacrificed, sent to drown as payment for the duplicitous nature of the town official. The Brothers Grimm, who popularized the *Pied Piper* story among many, put in print tales particularly harsh in the presentation of morality with consequences. In fact, **Willie Wonka and the Chocolate Factory** is another cruel exposé of handling sins (such as gluttony and sloth).

Rains' character in the TV special is the product of the social ills that permeate authority.

In one of Claude Rains' final movies, the actor ties the historical implications of colonial expansion and modern global imperialism together. *Lawrence of Arabia* is a grand David Lean piece of cinema that started the film career of Peter

British-Arab Summit/T.E. Lawrence *(far left)*

O'Toole. But, it's the Claude Rains character that ties much of the historical significance to the film. World War I was a turbulent time in British history. Proud that "the sun never set on the empire," their

King Herod *(actor role -1900)*

effort was not without cost. English diplomats spent much of their time keeping the colonies under the wing of their monarchy. This effort wandered from bravado to unrealistic expectation. Ultimately, the empire nearly collapsed by heavy-handed diplomacy that was archaic to the changing and modernizing times during and after World War II. The fictional character of Mr. Dryden in the film is a relatively small role. However, Rains captures the duplicity of his assignment by being at times deliberate and passive. He represents British prescence in an Arab world that has been fraught with centuries of infighting and religious unrest. His character is based on Sir Ronald Storrs, head of the Arab Bureau, and later Governor of Palestine. His whole purpose in diplomatic relations is to keep Turkish encroachment from destroying the Arab resolve in the region, while at the same time enforcing British rule in the area. It is a policy that was challenged by Israel's need for independence later in the century. Ghandi's India would fight this same battle with passive resistence. By 1950, the empire was a shadow of its former self. Mr. Dryden suceeds in keeping the Arab tribes at odds with each other but turns T. E. Lawrence into a martyred puppet. In the long run, this political effort was doomed to failure.

In his last film, Rains plays King Herod in *The Greatest Story Ever Told*. Here stands in Scripture the most ardent foe of the greatest disciple of Christian doctrine, Jesus of Nazareth. What a fitting conclusion for the actor who was the role model for tyranny and the status quo.

Claude Rains' characters are, in many ways, like-minded to the ideals expressed by British monarchs and nobles of a foregone era. Even Winston Churchill would fight fascism, in part, to protect the British Empire, and he was a product of his era. Through film, Rains captures this important part of history. Important because it comes in conflict with revolutionary thinking and the desire for modern individualization and enterprise, as opposed to the basic need for conquest of country that pervaded monarchies for centuries.

U.S. Republican Senator Everett Dirksen often referred to his Democratic colleages cordially as "the loyal opposition." He believed that, though both parties might

Everett McKinley Dirksen *(portrait)*

"The Loyal Opposition" at a Baseball Game in 1961
John Kennedy Entourage including Everett Dirksen *(second row)*

Senator Dirksen

disagree with issues of the day, they were faithfully bound to the principles of the Constitution. Dirksen played a key role in helping deliver the 1964 Civil Rights Bill for President Johnson to sign into law.

Claude Rains/Mr. Skeffington *(trailer)*

While either co-starring as an anti-revolutionary or a villainous person of nobility, Claude Rains' actual patriotism was authentic. He purposefully selected projects that captured the spirit of free-thinking Americans and people yearning for freedom around the world.

CHAPTER TWO

TRIUMPH OVER DISABILITY
Lionel Barrymore (1878-1954)

NO ACTING FAMILY IN HOLLYWOOD'S RICH HISTORY is considered more noble than the Barrymores. The son of actors, Maurice and Georgina, Lionel Barrymore's younger sister, Ethel, was an award-winning character actress. His brother, John, was famous for his magnificent profile. Several generations of Barrymores followed, and

Maurice Barrymore

Ethel Barrymore

Lionel Barrymore/Devil's Garden *(trailer)*

today, Drew Barrymore is a star that has come of age, and she is the great-neice of Lionel.

Lionel Barrymore began his acting career as a lead in silent movies and won a Best Actor award in 1930 for *A Free Soul.* His mention in this book is not for the lead parts he played, but for his great character roles that he would choose as he grew older. He became disabled because of a broken hip and persistant arthritis. The disease confined him to a wheelchair through all of his later career. What's amazing is the amount of work he received despite his disability, work that neither acknowledged his confinement nor cost him in quality of performance. His stardom mirrors the rise in power of Franklin Delano Roosevelt, whose disability due to polio also caused him confinement to a wheelchair. This did not stop our thirty-second President from being elected four times to high office, all the while battling the Great Depression of the 1930s and World War II in the 1940s. Unlike Barrymore, Roosevelt hid his disability from the American people; either embarrased by the disease's image or afraid the country would not have the

FDR Declaring War on Japan *(1941)*

Author Rudyard Kipling

confidence in his decision-making ability as president.

Obviously, Barrymore's "second" career was going to have an effect on the American psyche. He began his journey in all-star extravaganzas that featured top stars of the day...Greta Garbo, Jean Harlow, Joan Crawford, Wallace Beery, Marie Dressler, and his brother, John. In **Grand Hotel** and **Dinner at Eight**, he was the fellow with life-threatening illnesses, and this would prove valuable as his own personal drama began to emerge.

His role as Captain Disco in **Captains Courageous** was rugged, as it was idealistic, especially in his relationship with his son in the movie (played by Mickey Rooney). One might imagine that writer Rudyard Kipling had Barrymore in mind to play the part of a paternal father to all his fisherman, which included Spencer Tracy and John Carradine. These New England artisans were essential in providing food on the table of Depression-era folks across this country. He spends the last part of the film lecturing Melvin Douglas on the perils of Wall Street with sea-metaphors, aimed at teaching him about his spoiled son with whom he has become estranged. Though he was British, Rudyard Kipling's books translate well into great American classic movies. **Gunga Din** and **The Jungle Book** come to mind.

Playing a mentor came easy for Lionel Barrymore, and he was the obvious choice to play Dr. Gillespie in the **Dr. Kildare** series of films that were popular in the later thirties. The onset of his disability became apparent in these films, but Barrymore never lost the respect of the Lew Ayers character or the folks watching these movies.

You Can't Take It with You is a Pulitzer Prize-winning comedy by George S. Kaufman and Moss Hart. Director Frank Capra turned the book (and subsequent play) into the Best Picture of 1938. The center of this masterpiece is Lionel Barrymore's role of Grandpa Martin

Director Frank Capra

Vanderhof. He is the antithesis of corporate greed. He has little need for money, taxes, or government. A gentle anarchy reins over his household, but the heart of the play is the serious quest to be happy in this short life. Not even an obvious use of crutches can bring down the eccentric merriment of Vanderhof, and his giddy nature captures all who come in contact with him and his family.

In a role similar to the title character in **Here Comes Mr. Jordan**, Barrymore was selected to play the General, an angel-like character who protects our soldiers during World War II in the fantasy **A Guy Named Joe.** Sitting behing a conference desk, Barrymore is every bit

Lionel Barrymore/Armed Forces Radio Show

as authoritative as he needs to be in taking our fallen servicemen and re-assigning them as guardian angels over the military on Earth. In this parable, even angels that wander astray need guidance and counseling when returning to help the U.S. in its fight during World War II.

By the time *Duel in the Sun* was filmed, Barrymore would play all of his roles in his wheelchair. I think most film-goers understood that Lionel Barrymore would never walk on screen again. His appearance as a tough patriarch of a family torn by jealousy and competition didn't offer the pill of his own disability. It is a subject never approached to enhance the script.

Lionel Barrymore was a versatile actor and could easily play a villain. His annual radio appearance as Mr. Scrooge in Charles Dicken's *A Christmas Carol* didn't hurt.

His Mr. Potter in *It's a Wonderful Life* is deliciously evil in his efforts to rob the townsfolk of their property (maliciously referring to them as "yokels") and the James Stewart character, George Bailey, of his dignity. This movie is truly inspirational for many reasons. George Bailey feels trapped by a town that doesn't allow him to leave, first due to devotion to family and then through outside events that would shape his life. There is a run on the banks (presumebly because of the stock market crash of 1929). He is later classified as 4F because of a childhood accident that costs him his hearing in one ear, which eliminates any chance for Bailey to serve in the military. Filmed during World War II, even Mr. Potter displays patriotism as the head of the Draft Board. Bailey and Potter are relentless in their pursuits, and for most of the film, both fail miserably. What doesn't fail are the themes: Happiness begins at home, and everyone has worth in this most human experiment. These ideals are at the heart of this classic. This movie can't work without the perfect villain, and Barrymore embodies the essence of Mr. Potter.

Key Largo is the movie that comes closest to acknowledging Lionel Barrymore's illness. As an owner of a waterfront hotel, James Temple must confront his own frailty when incidents occur simultaneously. First, he must come to grips with the death of his son. Humphrey Bogart visits the inn to present Temple with his son's Medal of Valor, posthumously. This offers a little solace in light of his loss. Second, the hotel is overrun by gangsters, throwbacks to the era of Prohibition and content to live in the underbelly of American society. Finally, a hurricane threatens the community. The year of the movie, 1948, was before the accurate prognostication of when and where a hurricane might strike. Hunkering down where you lived was a way a life when calamaties hit close to home in Key Largo, Florida. Temple's confinement renders him helpless in his confrontation against the fugitives from the law and the natural catastrophe that might destroy his livelihood. It might have been the only time on film when Barrymore even mentions his wheelchair. But James Temple is still boisterous in spirit and a supportive confidant to the Bogart character.

When looking back at Lionel Barrymore's career, we see a charasmatic, larger-than-life performer that didn't let affliction diminish his role in Hollywood's studio era. What is never discussed is his pioneering effort to put disability on film. Without Barrymore, Harold Russell, fresh from military service from the Army (and an actual double amputee), may not have had the chance to play his almost autobiographic role of Homer Parrish, the discharged Navy sailor in *The Best Years of Our Lives*. The movie poigniantly explores the challenges loved ones face when living with persons with disabilities. Russell would win a record two Academy Awards for this role, though he never thought himself a real actor.

Anne Sullivan and Helen Keller

Hollywood would dramatize the issue of blindness in several pictures, including *Johnny Belinda*. Years later, Anne Bancroft

Helen Keller and
Mrs. Calvin Coolidge

and Patty Duke would star in *The Miracle Worker*, which examined the early life of Helen Keller, who overcame multiple disabilities with the help of teacher Anne Sullivan (also partially blind). She symbolizes triumph by battling extreme odds in order to live life to the fullest. Keller became a celebrated author and lecturer.

Marlee Matlin is a deaf actress, who starred in the 1986 motion picture *Children of a Lesser God*. The movie is essentially a love story with hearing impairment a subplot, rather than the focus.

Perhaps the finest movie of the genre is *My Left Foot*, which is the autobiographical story of Christy Brown, an Irishman with extreme cerebral palsy. Daniel Day-Lewis presents a graphic tale of survival and victory for the celebrated writer and artist in the 1989 film. Day-Lewis was honored with a well deserved Best Actor statuette.

John Garfield, Arthur Kennedy, Cliff Robertson, Geoffrey Rush, and others have sensitively dealt with the topics of physical and mental affliction on film. We now observe degenerative physical conditions not necessarily as a

Franklin Delano Roosevelt

hinderance but rather a challenging part of normal life. We see Lionel Barrymore providing the initial inspiration to a president. He also gave worldwide hope to generations of individuals, who otherwise might have hidden in the shadows because of disease and physical disorder. Barrymore was a humble sort, and he might have claimed that his wheelchair was simply a place he sat upon to do his craft.

Lionel Barrymore/Key Largo *(trailer)*

CHAPTER THREE

POWER OF THE ELUSIVE AMERICAN DREAM
Arthur Kennedy (1914-1990)

WHEN A GIFTED ACTOR IS INTERTWINED with the promise of a compelling script presented by the flat-out best writers of any century, expect remarkable results. Such is the story of Arthur Kennedy, who recited the words of the most important novelists of his time. Kennedy's gift was that he could play all-too-real characters that had many layers of emotion. These layers were subtle, which makes a visit to his motion pictures a must by even the most casual film-goer. This human "onion" involved himself with textured and complex parts through most of his career. We should also not forget the award-winning authors and playwrights that put on paper some of the finest material of the twentieth century. The bulk of Kennedy's most challenging roles were over a period of just twenty-five years. Yet, he was honored numerous times with accolades, which is quite an accomplishment. He was content in playing supporting parts of substance that would tap the intelligence of the motion-picture faithful and movie critics alike. One is never bored watching Arthur Kennedy in his element.

General George A. Custer *(drawing)*

Discovered by James Cagney, Kennedy would begin his career in 1940 playing his brother in **City for Conquest**. He would be typecast at times, playing the younger sibling of Kirk Douglas in **Champion**; and the older one of Frank Sinatra in **Some Came Running**. Kennedy made the most of these roles.

His early movies weren't particularly meaty. But, they were opportunities to work with some of the best in the business. In **They Died with Their Boots On**, Kennedy played opposite Errol Flynn in an inaccurate portrayal of General George A. Custer. Flynn's gallantry belied the truth that Custer was an opportunistic cavalry commander of the post-Civil War era, who used his hatred for "the Redskin" to promote his own political agenda. He was an aggressive leader that underestimated the resolve of the Sioux, Cheyenne, and Apache tribes, led by the fierce warrior, Crazy Horse, and Sioux patriarch, Sitting Bull. They slaughtered his regiment in what is known as "Custer's Last Stand." The movie paints Custer as an unwitting pawn in the attack by unscrupulous politicians that stir the Indians to battle. Kennedy has a small role of a coward who must join Custer in a tragic lesson of bravery.

High Sierra was a forties crime drama that was written by William R. Burnett. He is best known for the adaptations of his early works that spawned the gangster movie genre of the thirties, including **Little Caesar** and **Scarface**. His finest novel was turned into the *film noir* classic, **The Asphalt Jungle**. Burnett worked on *Sierra's* screenplay with John Huston.

Custer's Last Stand
(1905 stage production)

Humphrey Bogart, the star of the film, was no stranger to playing gangsters. His first big break came in *The Petrified Forest* at the suggestion of co-star Leslie Howard in 1936. His tough-guy image was already cemented by 1941, but his part as Roy "Mad Dog" Earle had an unexpected twist. Though a hard-

Arthur Kennedy/High Sierra *(trailer)*

ened killer, Earle is sensitive to the everyday folk with which he comes in contact and shows kindness to a stray pooch at his hideout. He even displays genuine disgust for the nickname he has inherited. Cast and critics lauded this performance as a new portrait of a mobster. Arthur Kennedy was cast as one of Earle's henchmen. It's easy to speculate about his particular appreciation of Bogart's versatility as an actor. Kennedy would "apply color" in his future roles, offering abundant conflict of purpose that made his characters more believable.

A chance to again work with Bogart in 1955 might have been a welcome opportunity for Kennedy. However, in *The Desperate Hours*, Bogart and Frederic March take most of the screen time in this hostage classic. Kennedy is relegated to the tedious job of tracking down the gangster played by Bogie. It's a thankless role that is never fleshed out in the way that is worthy of Kennedy's experience by that time as an actor. His task as sheriff has one important assignment...gunning down Bogart's character. This would be Humphrey Bogart's final role as a mobster.

During World War II, Arthur Kennedy was part of a fine ensemble cast assembled by director Howard Hawks that included John Garfield, Harry Carey, Gig Young and George Tobias for the Academy Award winning movie, *Air Force*. The film chronicles the exploits of a B-17 Flying Fortress engaged in combat, nicknamed the "Mary

Ann." Hawks used his expertise as a veteran in the Air Corps in providing some of the most vivid combat scenes ever directed up until this motion picture was made. In fact, the exterior of the actual bomber was used as part of the set. The poignancy of the story was not lost

The B-17 Flying Fortress Bomber

in that the movie was released roughly at the same time the plane was shot down during the very real Pacific Theatre campaign.

In 1947, Kennedy co-starred in a movie based on a true story of

U.S. Attorney General Homer Cummings

a 1924 incident involving Connecticut Attorney General Homer Cummings. The motion picture **Boomerang** is a gripping account about the murder of a minister and the subsequent accusation of a vagrant and discharged army soldier. Kennedy is cast as the accused individual who is later found innocent because of the thoroughness in the investigation by the attorney general and his staff. In truth, the National Commission on Law Observance and Enforcement praised Cummings for his efforts in this crime. He went on to become the fifty-fifth United

States Attorney General in the Franklin D. Roosevelt Administration. Serving with distinction, he strengthened the power of the Federal Bureau of Investigation (FBI), secured passage of key elements in the Lindbergh Law with relation to kidnapping, made bank robbery a federal crime, and cracked down on interstate transportation of stolen property. He also established Alcatraz Prison off San Francisco Bay. He is an example of an American who did plenty without the baggage of fame attached. Dana Andrews depicted Cummings, who acted as a technical advisor for the film.

Arthur Kennedy would occasionally step away from Hollywood to appear on Broadway. He began a long association with the most acclaimed Pulitzer Prize-winning American playwright of the second half of the

Playwright Arthur Miller

twentieth century, Arthur Miller. Miller captured our inner struggles with gripping exposés about everyday life. (Interestingly, he was married to Marilyn Monroe for a time.) Kennedy won a Tony Award for his fine performance in **Death of a Salesman**. He would go on to appear on stage in other Miller works, including the modern dramas, **All My Sons** and **The Price**, and the historical piece, **The Crucible**, which chronicles events that led to the Salem witch trials of the late 1700s. The play was actually written as a creative metaphor to McCarthyism (the cumpulsory practice of subpeonaed testimony before the Senate in the early 1950s). Kennedy's work on

Salem Witchcraft Trial *(drawing)*

stage examined the premise that the American dream could be elusive and that ordinary families could be dysfunctional because of burdens placed by a suburban society.

Kennedy starred in the uplifting **Bright Victory**, which tells the tale of a Southern soldier's sojourn to overcome physical blindness and, ultimately, defeat a metaphoric blindness to his racial bigotry. His Best Actor-nominated role was a breakthrough in his career but was overshadowed in a year (1951) when the Hollywood treatment of the Tennessee Williams Pulitzer Prize-winning play **A Streetcar Named Desire** was produced. As expected, *Streetcar* swept all acting categories at the Academy Awards, with the exception of Best Actor. Marlon Brando's explosive performance as Stanley Kowalski was bested by Kennedy mentor Humphrey Bogart in **The African Queen.** Bogie was not a fan of award shows and would always claim that, "the only true test would be to have every actor play *Hamlet…*!" He still offered a rousing acceptance speech for his statuette.

Arthur Kennedy did catch the attention of Tennessee Williams, and the masterful playwright would offer Kennedy a supporting role in the film adaptation of his semi-autobiographical **The Glass Menagerie** in 1950. Williams personalized much of his work, which include demented elements that ran through his extended family.

Anthony Mann was the expert director of the complex Western. His relationship with James Stewart is legendary. Mann would turn to Arthur Kennedy twice in the fifties to portray villains of subtle magnitude and immense charm. In **Bend of the River**, Kennedy would co-star as an outlaw and former post-Civil War Missouri raider in the model of Jesse James. He is a worthy adversary to Stewart, whose character has turned the corner on his own demons.

Playwright Tennessee Williams

Nobel Laureate Sinclair Lewis

More significant, *The Man from Laramie* is quintessential Anthony Mann, fashioning a western drama out of Shakespeare's *King Lear*. Kennedy's role is that of stepson to an iron-willed patriarch who spends most of his waking hours planning his real son's future. Kennedy's character, Vic Hansboro, is particularly tormented about not receiving the affection of his stepfather (played to perfection by Donald Crisp). Hansbro's bitterness leads to the unfortunate decision of running guns to renegade Indians in the county. James Stewart plays the Laramie, Wyoming, native searching for the reason why his brother's Army company was bushwhacked. Hansboro critically injures his stepfather and meets his own demise, not by the Stewart character but by the renegades. This motion picture hands Mann his crowning Western with a brutal portrait of frontier living during the late 1800s.

No one was more adroit than Arthur Kennedy in playing dysfunctional individuals in serene settings. His work with Arthur Miller and Tennessee Williams served him well. In *Peyton Place*, his character sexually abuses his stepdaughter, powerful and graphic material for the time, and a ferocious role. In *A Summer Place,* his failures as an innkeeper and husband lead to alcoholism and his wife's philandering. These pitiable *Places* produced vintage Kennedy performances.

One of his finest roles was in Sinclair Lewis' *Elmer Gantry*. The movie is a faithful adaptation of the novel that focuses on

Aimee Semple McPherson

American Revivalism of the 1920s. Burt Lancaster is Gantry, with Jean Simmons in a part modeled after the very real Aimee Semple McPherson. The evangelical crusades led by the revival movement that reached Middle America were stuff of legend, complete with parades, balloons, and a huge tent in the middle of town. Arthur Kennedy has a particular juicy role as reporter Jim Lefferts, who reports about the hypocrisy of evangelism and about the political hucksters that co-mingle with the movement. He also displays a curious admiration for the colorful individu-

Aimee Semple McPherson

als involved in the process. His gentlemanly feud with Gantry is a high point in the film. Sinclair Lewis is considered the most important writer in the first half of the twentieth century and was the first American awarded the Nobel Prize in Literature. His books foretold the dangers of the propensity for greed in a capitalist society.

Arthur Kennedy would again play a reporter in *Lawrence of Arabia* (the title character played by Peter O'Toole in his first film role). Kennedy portrays a character that resembles the real-life adventure journalist Lowell Thomas. Thomas made a name for himself as a war correspondent traveling with the man torn between countries during the Arab revolt at the outbreak of World War I. For his part, Thomas was the first known reporter embedded in a conflict. He was able to tour the U.S. and make a profitable living with the photographs and movie he developed at T. E. Lawrence's expense. Lawrence often referred to Thomas as a vulgar individual. Lowell Thomas suggested that journalism is essential in times of war. This was a compelling argument about the growing power of the press at the dawn of modern communication. Arthur Kennedy captures the vulgarity of the character, implying at Lawrence's funeral that his accounts alone were the most accurate with regards to the man's legacy. Incidentally, Kennedy re-dubbed the vocal track when the movie was restored shortly before his death.

Harold Robbins is arguably the best-selling author in the world, with over 750 millions copies of his writings sold. **Nevada Smith** was a 1966 adapted movie based on a popular charac-ter in his book, **The Carpetbaggers**. Steve McQueen plays the title role in the motion

Lowell Thomas and President Roosevelt

picture that approaches the subject of vengeance. A modern Western that is a precursor to the landmark **The Wild Bunch**, the film begins with the vicious killing of a settler and his Indian wife. Smith dedi-cates his life to the retribution of his parent's murder, and Karl Mal-den, Martin Landau, and Arthur Kennedy play the chased outlaws. The Kennedy character is ambivalent to the concerns of settlers and Indians in the territory but witnesses the killings. In a physical role, he is the likeable villain, Bill Bowdrie, who actually befriends Smith while on a chain gang. His fate is sealed because of guilt by associa-tion. After escaping their prison camp, Smith kills Bowdrie, which accidentally leads to the death of a Cajun girl that had become Smith's love interest. With the eventual guidance of a padre, Nevada Smith rethinks the vengeance business. He eventually replaces his feelings with a semblance of forgiveness, and he walks away from his final act of frontier justice. The movie contains a powerful message that culmi-nates in the salvation of the title character.

Arthur Kennedy remains a study of human complexity, and his portrayals would be the forerunner to the kinds of supporting roles popular in today's modern drama. The 1999 **American Beauty**, 2008

Revolutionary Road (from a book published in 1961), and other similar films might have included a part suited for Kennedy in his prime. One can speculate that, maybe only then, Arthur Kennedy might have received the Academy Award; the only elusive dream for this screen giant.

Arthur Kennedy Tombstone, Nova Scotia

CHAPTER FOUR

AN ADVOCATE AGAINST THE COMMUNIST THREAT
Ward Bond (1903-1960)

WHEN LOOKING BACK ON HOLLYWOOD'S GOLDEN AGE, some actors portray gallant heroes that give you a sense that our American history has been a noble and interesting journey. Every once in a while, a few actors rise above the parts they play and take stock in real-life roles that unfold to create history. Ward Bond did both. I might add his actions away from motion pictures may have fairly or unfairly tainted his screen image. At first glance, Bond's persona was rugged and gruff. This allowed him, however, to be typecast as individuals with authority. What emerged was a career of real and fictional characters that were primed to be at the center of this country's most determined hours.

Ward Bond/The Searchers *(trailer)*

Before being discovered, Bond was the starting linebacker for the most storied college football team in the twentieth century, the USC Trojans. His 1928 squad emerged as national champions, the first of many. One of his teammates became his lifelong friend, John Wayne (then known as Marion Morrison).

His film career in the thirties was uneven until 1939, when he started co-starring in a string of memorable movies that lasted his entire life. Amazingly, Ward Bond holds the record for appearing in more movies that have been nominated for Best Picture awards than any other actor in history. Those films include *It Happened One Night*, *You Can't Take It with You*, *Gone with the Wind*, *The Grapes of Wrath*, *The Maltese Falcon*, *Sergeant York*, *It's a Wonderful Life*, *The Quiet Man*, and *Mister Roberts.* He also appeared in more John Ford pictures than any other actor during the studio era of Hollywood. In addition to John Wayne, Bond could boast about being close friends with Clark Gable and director Howard Hawks. Though most of his roles were small and his acting ability limited, he secured a large number of parts as some of the "quiet" heroes in screen history. At the time of his death, Bond had appeared in over two hundred motion pictures.

In the 1939 drama *Drums along the Mohawk*, Bond plays Adam Helmer, a Revolutionary War hero. Helmer, a frontiersman, is actually credited in warning the people of German Flatts, New York of

Adam Helmer Gravesite, Cayuga County

an impending raid of Indians and Tories (British sympathizers). Due to his efforts, only two men were killed in the attack. Unfortunately, the true depiction in the novel and the subsequent film version differs, by giving the credit for this action to Gil Martin, a settler in the Mohawk Valley. This inaccurate discrepancy is the highlight in the movie. The heroic assignment was made by producer Darryl F. Zanuck to showcase the star of his film, Henry Fonda. Nonetheless, this was Bond's first foray towards playing men of substance.

Ward Bond was fortunate to appear in **Gone with the Wind**, playing a Union soldier that befriends Rhett Butler, played by Clark Gable. Though Yankee soldiers are looked upon with disdain throughout the film, Bond is the one sympathetic exception.

The Maltese Falcon is adapted from Dashiell Hammett's novel. Hammett is the pre-eminent hardboiled detective writer, who created the memorable characters Nick and Nora Charles (of the **Thin Man** series), Ellery Queen, and Sam Spade. Hammett was the mentor to legendary detective author, Raymond Chandler. He also had a thirty-year romantic affair with playwright, Lillian Hellman. Humphrey Bogart is Spade in the *Falcon* movie, which established him as a screen hero for the first time in his career. Ward Bond plays Homicide Detective Sgt. Tom Polhaus, who is Spade's friend. He is the one that asks Spade at the end of the movie about the nature of "the black bird." Spade replies: "It's the stuff dreams are made of…" It is one of Hollywood's legendary endings to a film and helped solidify the reputation of a movie studio as a "dream factory." It is also interesting to note that Polehaus would probably go on to round up the talented cast of cutthroats that included Sidney Greenstreet, Peter Lorre, Mary Astor, and Elisha Cook Jr.

Heavyweight Champion
John L. Sullivan

Bond's husky build served him well as John L. Sullivan, the initial Heavyweight Champion of Gloved Boxing. In **Gentleman Jim**, Errol Flynn stars as Jim Corbett, the boxer that legitimized the practice as sport by primarily boxing under the Marques of Queensbury rules. Among other things, the rules (written in 1865 by

John L. Sullivan *(during a prizefight)*

John Graham Chambers and published in 1867) dictate that 1) matches be held in a specified ring, 2) the length of the rounds be three minutes, 3) a boxer be allowed a ten count to get up from a punch, and 4) gloves be used during the bout. In reality, Sullivan had fought under such rules, but he is generally regarded as a "bare knuckles" champion. When Corbett defeated Sullivan in the twenty-first round of their

U.S. Marshal Morgan Earp

prizefight held in New Orleans in 1892, he announced to the crowd, "If I had to get licked, I'm glad… it was by an American." Sullivan was inducted to the International Boxing Hall of Fame in 1990 as part of their original class. Ward Bond is cagey and flamboyant in the role.

In **My Darling Clementine**, Bond played Morgan Earp, the real brother of Wyatt, who participated in the gunfight at the O.K. Corral in 1880s Tombstone, Arizona. In addition to brother Virgil and Doc Holliday, Morgan was wounded in the confrontation. He later died from retaliation by supporters of the Clanton gang as a result of the gunfight. The attack narrowly missed killing Wyatt Earp. Wyatt avenged his brother's death by murdering anyone he felt had been involved during a three-week rampage.

Ward Bond really excelled in World War II pictures. He appeared in *A Guy Named Joe*, *The Fighting Sullivans*, and *Mister Roberts*.

Ward Bond/A Guy Named Joe *(trailer)*

Bond also co-starred in the movie *They Were Expendable*, a fictionalized account about the importance of PT boats and their value as viable naval craft during the war in the Pacific. The craft was instrumental in the evacuation of General Douglas MacArthur from the Philippines. Bond played a member of the squadron.

PT Boat Naval Poster

Many consider Ward Bond's best film to be *Operation Pacific*. In the motion picture, he portrays a fictional submarine commander, based on incidents involving the real Captain Howard W. Gilmore of the USS *Growler*. Gilmore chose to make the supreme sacrifice while protecting his men when his sub came under fire. Clearing the deck and ordering his second-in-command to "take her down," he saved all on board during the confrontation. Gilmore was unable to reach the deck below, but during the attack, his sub sank a

Japanese freighter and crippled another with torpedo fire. Captain Gilmore was posthumously awarded the Medal of Honor for his gallantry and valor. To honor Gilmore, all sub captains to this day initiate their dives with the phrase, "Take her down." Bond modeled his skipper after Gilmore, and at his side is John Wayne, who follows that fateful order to save the damaged sub. This moment in the film is a bittersweet tribute.

Navy Medal of Honor

Director John Ford made a critically acclaimed trilogy of Westerns that honored the army cavalry for its contributions and provided the first sympathetic portrait of the American Indian. These movies were Hollywood's first attempt at rectifying the myths created by earlier films and storied accounts. The initial film in this trilogy is **Fort Apache**. The cavalry of the post-Civil War era actually dealt more with the Sioux and less with the Apache. However, more charismatic leaders, such as Geronimo and Cochise, led the Apache tribes. The movie's premise is that broken treaties by the U.S. Government led to deadly skirmishes initiated by Cochise and others. Bond plays a sgt. major that dies out of duty to country, despite the government's broken promises. In reality, Cochise accepted the ultimate relegation of his people to designated reservations.

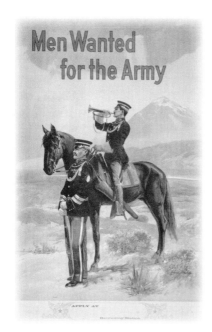

U.S. Cavalry Recruitment Poster

Ironically, Bond's most lasting tribute is from a movie grounded in fantasy. **It's A Wonderful Life** has many memorable performances; among them, a cab driver named Ernie (played by the genial actor Frank Faylen), and cop known as Bert (a rare Ward Bond comedic turn). They are good friends to George Bailey (the Jimmy Stewart role), and show great empathy for his desire to leave his hometown to explore the world. In one particular poignant moment, Bert and Ernie serenade George and his new wife, played by Donna Reed. They also pin posters of exotic sites around their new home. Decades later, Jim Henson would immortalize these softhearted pals by naming two of his muppets, Bert and Ernie. Ernie croons to a generation of youngsters in a memorable episode of the Emmy winning **Sesame Street**, inviting a rubber duckie to bath time. Hygiene is a typical everyday subject that Henson focused on in his efforts to educate youngsters on 1970s public television.

The politics of post World War II would creatively damage Hollywood as a result of the Cold War that developed between the Soviet Union and their former allies. The Motion Picture Alliance for the Preservation of American Ideals was formed to defend the film industry against the infiltration of Communism. Members of the group were willing to testify before the House of Representative's Committee on Un-American Activities (HUAC) to name actors, directors, and writers that were possibly associated with Communist organizations in the U.S. The Alliance positioned itself as a group determined to protect patriotic ideals in film. Ward Bond was an active member, and he saw his association as an alignment with the many roles he portrayed. Other members of the group included his pal John Wayne, Walt Disney, and Ronald Reagan. Novelist, playwright, and screenwriter Ayn

Ronald Reagan/Berlin Wall

Rand, a Soviet who emigrated to the U.S., considered herself the foremost moral authority on the subject of Communism. She wrote in a pamphlet for the Alliance, "The purpose of the Communists in Hollywood is...to corrupt our moral premises by corrupting non-political movies—by introducing small casual bits of propaganda into innocent stories." She went on to write that "The principle of free speech doesn't require that we furnish Communists with the means to preach their ideas and does not imply that we owe them jobs and support to advocate our own destruction at our own expense." These words were damming at a time when our country feared enemy nations that had the capability to build the atomic bomb.

Gale Sondergaard/The Letter *(trailer)*

The problem is that any names mentioned before the HUAC would have an adverse consequence on their subsequent careers in Hollywood. Blacklisting became a common practice for those trying to find work in light of the hysteria caused by the "red scare." Careers were ruined, some for decades and others permanently, for an unwillingness to participate in the "witch hunt" that permeated Washington D.C. Actors, such as Gale Sondergaard and Larry Parks, and writers, Dalton Trumbo and Dashiell Hammett were creatively finished simply because of their refusal to "name names." Accused of being a Communist, actor Lee J. Cobb was one of the few able to resume his career after he decided to give testimony (he had refused for two years).

Ward Bond was reviled in some Hollywood circles for his outspoken commitment against the perceived Communist threat. Bond remained defiant until the end of his life over the issue. His last film **Rio Bravo**, starring John Wayne and directed by Howard Hawks, was produced as a direct response to the making of **High Noon**. They considered this motion picture an allegory for blacklisting in Hollywood and a direct critique of McCarthyism. Bond also actively campaigned to elect Richard Nixon, a champion against the Soviet cause, in his 1960 presidential run. However, Bond died of a sudden heart attack days before John F. Kennedy narrowly defeated Nixon.

President Nixon, John Wayne and Henry Kissinger

Eventually, Nixon was elected President, and in 1972, made a monumental visit to the People's Republic of China. This trip was an important first step that led to the normalization of relations between our countries. He further negotiated U.S./Soviet *detente*, which eventually put in place a limitation of strategic arms between the two countries. Actor-turned-President Ronald Reagan would effectively initiate the end of the Cold War by ordering Soviet Premier Mikhail Gorbachev to "tear down that wall" that separated West and East Germany in his 1987 remarks at Berlin's Brandenburg Gate. John Wayne has been lionized as a great American, with an airport and schools named in his honor.

The Berlin Wall
(symbol of Communism)

Former President Harry Truman in 1959 denounced the HUAC as "the most un-American thing in our country today." Ward Bond was a willing pawn in our government's organized campaign to use Hollywood for the creation of hysteria within our citizenry. Maybe it's time to refocus on the patriotic intent of Ward Bond and others, who were derided for their obviously destructive political beliefs, at a time when no one emerged a winner. His many gallant portrayals in his film career offer an attractive case in his defense.

Ward Bond/They Were Expendable *(trailer)*

CHAPTER FIVE

TALL IN THE SADDLE
Walter Brennan (1894-1974)

I WOULD ARUGE, THE WEST WAS WON in films by the likes of Gary Cooper, John Wayne, Randolph Scott, and William Boyd. At a closer glance, the leather, sun-drenched face that most commonly helped tame the wild frontier was that of Walter Brennan. Brennan is the most honored American male actor in history, winning three of the first five Supporting Actor awards. He also embodies any individual that may have been born around and west of the Mississippi.

Looking far older than his years, Brennan could be called upon to play roles that were based in fact or fiction.He seemingly lived throughout the nineteenth century and the fight for this country's quest to reach "from sea to shining sea"...at least on celluloid.

Walter Brennen/Meet John Doe *(trailer)*

The movie Western has its roots around the birth of motion pictures at the turn of the twentieth century, with the production of *The Great Train Robbery* in 1903. Based on actual facts, the picture ran twelve minutes and is important in the development of nar-

Edison Movie Studios *(circa 1910)*

rative in film. It captured the imagination of audiences that marveled at the innovation of visual storytelling. Thomas Edison created the first movie studio, and The Edison Company produced the picture. *A Bird in a Guilded Cage* in 1908 is another period narrative piece produced by The Edison Company.

Nineteenth century frontier history was initially documented by stories verbally passed on through generations of recollection and less factual sensationalized accounts in printed press reports from the East. Publisher Horace Greeley's suggestion to "go West young man" was made, in part, to receive stories of the growing territories and help increase circulation of his successful newspaper business. With the rise in land grants to the railroad industry, news could travel faster about the trials and tribulations of the California Gold Rush, the Civil War, cattle drives, wagon train

A Bird In A Guilded Cage *(scene two)*

accounts, and other major frontier tales that fascinated readers.

The motion picture Westerns made during the studio era that stretched into the 1960s also weren't necessarily accurate, as they were compelling stories of struggle during the U.S. frontier of the 1800s. There were cowboys, settlers, ranchers, gunslingers, gamblers, marshals, and outlaws. Throughout his long acting career, Walter Brennan played them all.

In *Come and Get It*, Brennan cemented his place in screen history by winning the very first award for Best Supporting Actor in 1936. Set in nineteenth century Wisconsin, the film put Brennan

Newspaper Publisher
Horace Greeley

in a familiar role as a buddy of the head of a lumberjack dynasty. The film is based on a book by Edna Ferber, the Pulitzer Prize-winning novelist, noted for fleshing out strong characters in her writings. Ferber lived most of her life in Wisconsin and was born in the latter part of the nineteenth century. The adaptation of her sprawling tale *Cimarron* was the first screen Western to win a Best Picture Award in 1930. She was honored with her own postage stamp in 2002.

Kentucky is a Hatfield and McCoy tale set against the backdrop of the Bluegrass State's fascination with horse racing. This film displayed Walter Brennan's depth as a dramatic actor, for which his peers honored him a second time with a golden statuette.

The fourth screen adaptation of America's premier author, Mark Twain's *The Adventures of Tom Sawyer* was Brennan's next project. Twain's fascination with the mighty Mississippi River and those who lived around it is legendary. Featured in the cast were rich portraits of the title character, along with Huckleberry Finn, Becky Thatcher, Injun Joe, and the local drunkard, Muff Potter (falsely accused of

Author Mark Twain *(left)*   Huckleberry Finn *(drawing)*

murder). It is the Potter role that Brennan brings to life with empathy and humor. His acquittal of the capital crime captures the Midwestern value of fairness in the justice system that hoped to settle raids along the border state of Missouri after the Civil War.

1940 was a banner year for Walter Brennan. In **Northwest Passage**, he plays the friend of real life adventurer Major Rogers, who discovered the Northwest Trail to the Pacific Ocean in the mid eighteenth century. Brennan's character was a fictional composite of the kind of local New Hampshire woodsman that joined Roger's Rangers in their battles during the French and Indian Wars. It was these early struggles that strengthened the resolve of ordinary men and challenged their curiosity to explore the West.

His next performance many regard as Brennan's finest—that of Judge Roy Bean in **The Westerner**. Essentially a villain, Bean's dispensation of frontier justice was often swift and cruel. Brennan created a character that was flawed and dealt with issues as homesteading and horse stealing. In real life, Judge Roy Bean was an eccentric saloon owner, justice of the peace, and the self-proclaimed "only law west

Judge Bean "Courthouse" Saloon/Langtry, Texas *(circa 1900)*

of the Pecos." An admirer of real-life, nineteenth century performer Lily Langtry, Bean often dispensed his courtroom decisions from his saloon, usually in the form of a fine since his town had no jail or courthouse. Bean died peacefully in bed in 1903. In the movie, Judge Bean dies in a ruse to meet Langtry after being shot by Gary Cooper's character. In fact, Cooper was against doing the movie since Judge Roy Bean was the central figure in the film. Cooper's instincts were right. Walter Brennan essentially steals the movie and a record third Academy Award.

Sergeant York is a movie about the most decorated American in World War I. Gary Cooper landed the role of Alvin C. York, originally a conscientious objector because of

Sgt. York/Cornay, France *(1919)*

his religious beliefs as a Christian. Born in the backwoods of Tennessee, York reaches his decision to defend his country with the help of his pastor, played by Brennan. In a small role, Brennan offers great compassion and dignity. The movie takes its time in York's transformation from his objection to war to celebrated hero. Seven members of the 328th Infantry under his command captured 132 German soldiers near Cornay, France. General John J. Pershing awarded York the U.S. Medal of Honor and the Distinguished Service Cross. The French Republic awarded him the Croix de Guerre and the Legion of Honor. Italy presented him the Croce di Guerra. Alvin York was also promoted from corporal to sergeant as part of his honor after the Great War. Brennan's role was that of a weathered man of the cloth, brought up with nineteenth century values that he imparts to his congregation, which includes the York family. Again, he was nominated for a Best Supporting Actor award for this gentle characterization.

Alvin C. York Request for Army Discharge (1917)

Walter Brennan occassionally played in contemporary films. Usually in comedic buddy parts, he appeared with Cooper in **Meet John Doe** and with Humphrey Bogart in Ernest Hemmingway's **To Have and Have Not**. He is also the scout that discovers Lou Gehrig in **Pride of the Yankees.** In a later role, Brennan is the moral backbone to Spencer Tracy in **Bad Day at Black Rock**. The story is about a fictional town filled with unsavory and shady inhabitants that harbor a gruesome secret...the murder of an innocent Japanese American during the height of World War II, despite the fact that the victim's son is a decorated hero.

However, Brennan was at his best in Westerns. In the 1946 production of **My Darling Clementine**, he plays the real life patriarch of the Clanton gang that challenges Wyatt Earp and Doc Holliday in Tombstone, Arizona. The actual gunfight at the O.K.Corrall happened on October 26, 1881, and was born out of a gambling quarrel between Holliday and the younger Ike Clanton. Both were prone to drinking, and each had bad tempers. Since Earp and his brothers (Virgil and Morgan) were "the law," legend paints the Clantons as villainous cattle rustlers that used force to control the town. In fact, the Clantons were amiable ranchers that mingled well with the townsfolk. Members of the Clanton gang, Frank and Tom McLaury, also sided with the ranchers in the interest of development. The Clanton association with outlaws of the time and the accidental killing of Tombstone Marshal Fred White, did nothing to endear the law with the area ranchers. The movie suggests the legend played better to audiences, and Brennan obliged by playing "Old Man" Clanton with appropriate menace. The film's climax is the West's most famous gunfight (which actually took place at Harwood's Lumber at the rear of the corral).

Old Man Clanton
(only known photo)

Director Howard Hawks brought out the best in Walter Brennan in movies such as **To Have and Have Not**. In **Red River**, Hawks creates a fictional account of the first cattle drive along the Chisholm Trail (from Texas to Kansas). This sprawling Western is filled with grey-area characters in which decisions made along the trail were tough and potentially dangerous. Brennan plays the cook that ultimately must betray his friend portrayed by John Wayne. Wayne is a tough son-of-a-gun, unsympathetic to human weakness. It is his tyrannical adherance to perfec-

The Klondike Trail

tion that clouds his judgment along the trail that ultimately leads to a *coup*. The movie is a sagebrush **Mutiny on the Bounty** with similar results. Walter Brennan acts as the conscience to Wayne's Thomas Dunson. Through unwavering advice by Brennan, Dunson ultimately avoids tragic consequences at the film's conclusion.

Alaska Gold Rush Mining Camp
(circa 1900)

Tragedy is at the heart of **The Far Country**, a cautionary tale of lawlessness that pervaded the Alaskan frontier during the Klondike Gold Rush of the 1890s. Brennan is the amiable friend, Ben Tatum, to James Stewart's hero, Jeff Webster. Tatum is prone to poor judgment which costs the character his

Col. Stewart awarded
France's Croix De Guerre

life. Webster avenges his friend and helps settle the lawless territory in the process. Anthony Mann was the most successful director in bringing out the toughness in any Stewart character. Their collaboration in Westerns display on film the grit and determination a hero could muster in territories where law and order is scarce. Walter Brennan rarely died in his movies. The death of Ben Tatum jolted audiences watching the film. Anthony Mann was at his best when directing movies where tragedy pervaded a potaganist's soul.

James Stewart in real life was far from his easy-going and self-righteous persona that was created by films he made prior to World War II. In fact, Stewart was the highest ranking military actor of his generation. He flew in dangerous combat missions during World War II and eventually achieved the rank of brigadier general. His movie contract expressly prohibited the mention of his heroics in the Armed Services to promote his film career.

The 1950s ended with one of Howard Hawk's best Westerns, **Rio Bravo**. Walter Brennan, by this time, noticeably limped. Hawks did not shy from this fact, naming the Brennan character "Stumpy." John Wayne, who starred and produced the film, teamed with Hawks to present a movie in which the hero faces his demons by standing down the outlaws bent on freeing a jailed murderer. Wayne's sheriff was brave, if outnumbered. And with the help of a young gunslinger, an alcoholic friend, a Mexican hotel proprieter, and his feisty lame deputy, Wayne prevails in defeating the bad guys. It's a simple, effective Western. Television's ***Gunsmoke*** would serve a helping of this message each week during the fifties and sixties.

The career of Walter Brennan is the tale of the days before and after the Civil War. His rare forays into the twentieth century were pure diversions that put on display his gifted acting ability. He is part of a bygone era. Thankfully, the majority of his celluloid work offers a constant reminder that the U.S. frontier was won on the backs of the little man determined to explore the hills, mountains, and prairies, which, sadly, is captured today only in our most patriotic music and stories passed down through a dwindling generation of Americans.

Walter Brennan/Rio Bravo *(trailer)*

CHAPTER SIX

1939...HOLLYWOOD'S CROWN JEWEL

Thomas Mitchell (1892-1962)

HOLLYWOOD COULD NOT HAVE WRITTEN A BETTER SCRIPT for what was to transpire in the golden year of 1939. At the time, movies were not the most pressing thing on the mind of most Americans. The growing Nazi threat had culminated in *blitzkrieg,* the modern mechanized lightning attacks on Poland and other countries in Eastern Europe, which forced France and England into another major war. Yet, isolationism was the word of the day around the U.S. of the late 1930s. Two leading proponents of isolationist policies were important figures at home and abroad. In America, aviation pioneer Charles Lindbergh vocalized the need for the U.S. to stay out a war across the Atlantic. Abroad, Joseph Kennedy, father of future President John F. Kennedy, was the ambassador to Britain and a noted isolationist. In retrospect, both

Isolationism Protest, Washington D.C.

Author Margaret Mitchell

couldn't have been more wrong when researching through the historical microscope that points to the Holocaust and other Nazi atrocities. In truth, Americans were not ready to fight in another war. Psychologically, mothers couldn't put another generation of youth in harm's way, and in practice, our military arsenal at the time was frankly substandard. The Great Depression had also ravaged this country economically for almost a decade. We were also almost two years away from the attack on Pearl Harbor.

What transpired from MGM, Paramount, Warner Bros., Columbia, RKO, and other film studios was an unparalleled collection of films that would not be matched in any other year of movie-making. First and foremost, Hollywood was abuzz over the impending release of the colossal epic love story set to the backdrop of the Civil War, **Gone with the Wind** (adapted from Margaret Mitchell's novel). Everyone in the business believed that one actor should inevitably play Rhett Butler: Clark Gable. However, gossip columnists speculated that the all-important female protagonist of Scarlett O'Hara could go to any number of leading ladies of the day, including Bette Davis and Katharine Hepburn. No doubt, the movie would sweep every major film award of the day. But, 1939 proved to be a year of memorable decisions with regards to the business of filmmaking. The first shock came when little known English actress Vivian Leigh was

Vivian Leigh/Gone With The Wind
(trailer)

selected to play the coveted role of Scarlett. Even more surprising is that she was up to the challenge, putting on celluloid perhaps the greatest female screen performance in history.

What has this to do with Thomas Mitchell? A little patience, please! Movie pundits could not be more wrong in their prognostication for what was to emerge in 1939. While David O. Selznick was producing his Civil War epic, other groundbreaking motion pictures were in production. Many top actors in Hollywood were also working in some of the finest roles of their careers. James Stewart captured our patriotism in **Mr. Smith Goes to Washington**.

Bette Davis and Errol Flynn/Private Lives Of Elizabeth & Essex *(trailer)*

Bette Davis consoled her loss of playing Scarlett by taking the role of Queen Elizabeth I in **The Private Lives of Elizabeth and Essex** (with Errol Flynn as her romantic counterpart). Greta Garbo was concluding her career in the classic, *Ninotchka*. Two emerging actors were showcased in hot properties: John Wayne in **Stagecoach** and Laurence Olivier in **Wuthering Heights**. A movie adaptation of John Steinbeck's novella **Of Mice and Men** was skillfully filmed. And, Kate Hepburn was in the process of a major Hollywood comeback on Broadway, starring in and securing the rights to **The Philadelphia Story**.

Looking back to that year, no one would have imagined that one movie would long be remembered over all others by an entire generation known as baby boomers. And, that movie was not **Gone with the Wind**. The advent of television in the fifties allowed youngsters to fall in love with a mythical place created by a writer from the turn of the century. L. Frank Baum's **The Wizard of Oz** remains the most enduring picture of 1939. Children of the 1950s and 1960s were annually allowed to visit a place that lay "Over the Rainbow" through the magic of television, making this movie a perennial favorite. MGM producers were unhappy about the motion picture at the time for a variety of reasons. First, they were unable to obtain the rights to the most popular child star of the thirties, Shirley Temple. They settled on Judy Garland for the lead role. Also, executives knew then that any movie that would come out in 1939 would lie in the shadow of *Gone with the Wind*. Finally, the supporting male leads were at best, a combination of journeyman hoofers in Ray Bolger, Bert Lahr, and Jack Haley, hardly box-office draws. Today, *The Wizard of Oz* is the most remembered film of that magical year.

Wizard Of Oz/Tin Man
(circa 1900 photo)

Don't worry...I haven't forgotten Thomas Mitchell... The 1939 Oscar ceremony was nothing short of astonishing in its results. Apart from the expected wins for Vivian Leigh and *Gone with the Wind*,

Hattie McDaniel

a variety of surprises occurred. Selznick had a favorite in the supporting actress category... Olivia De Havilland. When the award was presented, a barrier of monumental importance was broken. Hattie McDaniel became the first "person of color" to win an Academy Award. It would be almost another two decades before another African American would even be nominated, Dorothy Dandridge, and almost twenty-five years later that a black actor would even win the award, Sidney Poitier. We were even ten years away from the first African American baseball player in the major leagues. Yet, there stood Hattie, accepting her statuette for her role as Mammy.

The Best Actor award shaped up to be a competitive fight between James Stewart and Clark Gable. Stewart had delivered the performance of a lifetime, and Gable was in a movie for the ages. Looking back, two other actors nominated could have won the statuette. Mickey Rooney was voted the number-one box-office draw that year at the tender age of nineteen, due largely in part to his *Andy Hardy* series, and his likeable pairings with Judy Garland in a variety of films. He was nominated for *Babes in Arms*. Laurence Olivier, who many consider the greatest actor of the twentieth century (for my money, I'll take Spencer Tracy), had his breakthrough role in *Wuthering Heights*. He would go on to be nominated ten times for Best Actor, more than any male star in history. However, when the envelope was opened, the winner was Robert Donat for his performance in *Goodbye, Mr. Chips*. He was the "other" British nominee who was the forerunner of understated actors from England that include Paul Scofield. Not well known to American audiences, Donat had been well respected on the British stage for years.

Which brings us to Thomas Mitchell! Mitchell was in no less than FIVE of the great films of 1939. He was quite simply the hardest working actor of the year…and voted the Best Supporting Male Actor of 1939. Before this special year, he was hardly memorable in the roles he played. Mitchell was noticeably good, playing the doctor in 1937's *The Hurricane*. But, despite a twenty-five-year career, only two movies really stand out after 1939: the unforgettable 1946 *It's a Wonderful Life* where he played the forgetful Uncle Billy and the controversial 1952 *High Noon*

Thomas Mitchell/High Barbaree (trailer)

as Mayor Jonas Henderson. The benchmark of his career is that he is the first actor to win an Oscar, a Tony, and an Emmy.

Quite frankly, 1939 should have been the year of Walter Brennan's record-setting reception of a third film award. Incidentally, Brennan wasn't even nominated for anything. Brian Aherne was busy stealing *Juarez* from screen legend Paul Muni. Brian Donlevy was masterful

Gone With The Wind *(trailer)*

in the classic, ***Beau Jeste.*** And, Claude Rains was chewing the scenery with James Stewart in ***Mr. Smith Goes to Washington.*** But I digress…

A first-generation Irish American actor, Thomas Mitchell is the crown jewel of 1939 Hollywood. Not only did he play the father of Scarlett O'Hara in ***Gone with the Wind***, a part he masters with broad strokes embodied by the tragic consequences of the South losing the Civil War, but he also is the most vocal member of the "Fourth Estate" in ***Mr. Smith Goes to Washington***. Mitchell lectures Jefferson Smith (the Stewart character) about the perils of life in Washington's inner circle. As a member of the press, he is both cynical and honest, providing added humor to the storyline.

Mitchell was also in the Cary Grant minor classic ***Only Angels Have Wings***, a forerunner to World War II movies about aviation. It tells the brave story of what it means to be a pilot in the 1930s. Mitchell has a memorable "death scene," surrounded by friends who co-habitate this tumultuous work environment. Movies like this spoke of the need for the U.S. to step up its air force with a looming war on the horizon.

Hunchback Of Notre Dame *(drawing)*

Forgotten in a slew of great 1939 performances, is Thomas Mitchell's role in the Victor Hugo adaptation of *The Hunchback of Notre Dame*. The film stars the incredibly versatile Charles Laughton. Mitchell is the narrator, named Clopin Trouillefou, in this fictional piece. An unwitting ally to Quasimodo, (the hunchback), Clopin proves heroic in fighting to the death in order to protect Esmerelda, the love interest from afar of the title character.

In the end, Thomas Mitchell won the Best Supporting Award for none of these roles. These movies could have been distributed in subsequent years, and he would have received numerous accolades. His award-winning performance as Doc Boone, the alcoholic physician, was Mitchell at his best. He varied his portrayal (innocuous and commanding) as he traveled along in the most memorable *Stage-*

Stagecoach *(circa 1890 photo)*

coach ride in celluloid history. The film has rich performances from a strong cast of character actors that includes Claire Trevor, John Carradine, Andy Devine, Donald Meek, and George Bancroft. However, it was Mitchell's doctor that framed the rugged nature of the West in the latter nineteenth century. His delivery of a baby under primitive conditions (as he did in *The Hurricane*) is alternately silly and truthful. John Ford's sagebrush classic made John Wayne a star and an icon for decades to come. Thomas Mitchell knew where he stood in the movie and delivered perfection. That is what John Ford Westerns demanded, and why he would win four Best Director Awards of his own.

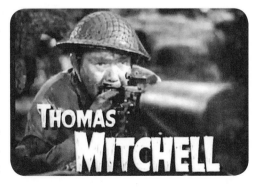

Thomas Mitchell/Bataan *(trailer)*

There were other notable Thomas Mitchell performances on the horizon, including **Our Town** in 1940, again playing a doctor. He also co-starred in a couple of World War II films...**Bataan** in 1943 and **The Fighting Sullivans** in 1944. In the latter motion picture, he co-starred as the real-life father of doomed brothers who fought

Sullivan Brothers, U.S.S. Juneau

bravely during action in the Pacific Theatre against the Japanese. What is particularly tragic is that all five siblings, assigned to the USS *Juneau*, were killed during the same incident. Because of the notoriety, the U.S. Government changed its policy of male family members fighting in the same battle. A related story is the subject of the 1998 movie **Saving Private Ryan**.

The year 1939 is fascinatingly historic in its presentation of cinema. In subsequent years, Americans would concern themselves with the real drama of World War II. Movies would take a back seat to the fight against real villains by the actual heroes that defined a generation, from Pearl Harbor to D-Day and through the Battle of the Bulge and Iwo Jima. Newscaster Tom Brokaw would later call these brave souls the greatest of the twentieth century.

Theodore Roosevelt Jr. Gravesite, Normandy

Thomas Mitchell might have completed "the hat trick" if Toto, Dorothy's dog in *Oz*, had fatefully pulled the curtain to find that he was the wizard in the film's final scenes, instead of jovial actor Frank Morgan. That said, what a year Mitchell chose to call his own.

CHAPTER SEVEN

HISTORY'S FOOTNOTE
John Carradine (1906-1988)

JOHN CARRADINE IN FILM COULD BE SURLY, boastful, a coward, and a varmint. This is not to say that he always played villains. American history is filled with people that were contemptible and vain. Their stories are seldom told, or have unfolded in the shadow of great individuals. However, without acknowledging "human asterisks" of eras gone by, much of our past would remain relatively incomplete. For example, anyone can tell you that Mrs. O'Leary's cow started the Great Chicago Fire, but who remembers the victims of the devastation. Most Presidents of the U.S. have documented lists of their accomplishments. Yet, their administrations are filled with little-known Cabinet Members who actually

Great Chicago Fire *(artist depiction)*

carried out the day-to-day agenda. Ann Frank is the face of the Holocaust, which took the lives of six million without a name, because of a simple diary she kept. Shelly Winters was honored for portraying little-remembered Mrs. Van Daan, one of the eight Jews hiding with the Frank family in an attic, attempting to survive in Nazi-occupied Amsterdam. John Carradine spent an entire career in roles than can be construed as footnotes to history. His contribution is immeasurable.

Ann Frank House, Amsterdam

One of his first important screen appearances was that of Long Jack in the Rudyard Kipling adaptation of **Captains Courageous**. He was a tempestuous fisherman who had little patience for the schooner's newest member, a spoiled rich youngster played by Freddie Bartholomew. Fetched from the sea, Bartholomew learns simple valuable lessons about the democratic life aboard a Gloucester's fishing vessel. Carradine portrays an adult that hasn't learned life's lessons as well as others, though his work ethic could not be questioned.

Much of the movie **Jesse James** is quite candidly inaccurate. The romanticizing of this secession-minded outlaw is shameful. Along with his brother Frank, he was a bank-robbing outlaw that graduated to the banditry of stagecoaches and trains. He was not above murdering anyone who got

John Carradine/Captain's Courageous (trailer)

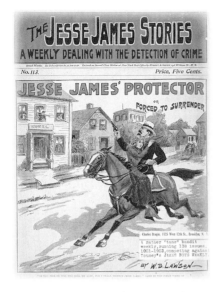

Jesse James *(dime novel)*

Outlaw Robert Ford

in his way, and he was far from the "Robin Hood of the West" that the movie glamorizes. Nor was he a wronged Confederate out for frontier justice. What's true is that President Ulysses S. Grant put a five-thousand-dollar bounty on the outlaw's head, and a cowardly member of his gang, Bob Ford, shot James in the back at his home for the reward money. John Carradine played Ford.

THE STAGE.

Stagecoach *(cartoon drawing)*

In the John Ford classic **Stagecoach**, Carradine plays a gambler and Southern gentleman named Hatfield. During an Apache attack, Hatfield makes an agonizing decision to use his last bullet on one of the female passengers to avoid her being captured and potentially scalped. He is killed before he fires the gun. Director Ford was quick to visualize the bleak choices that needed to be made on the frontier.

Part of an ensemble cast, John Carradine was in the first disaster movie **Five Came Back**, which also starred a virtually unknown Lucille Ball in 1939. Carradine plays a bounty hunter that is a passenger on an airplane that crashes in the Amazon. Though he is extraditing an anarchist that has killed a politician in an unmentioned South American country, the disaster turns Carradine's character from a person of authority to a rather weak individual. The anarchist becomes the decision-maker as to who should survive the ordeal and emerges a redemptive soul.

Drums along the Mohawk tells the story of settlers that had to endure the British, Tory (British sympathizers), and Mohawk attacks in pre-revolutionary New York. Carradine was cast as real-life Tory ranger, William Caldwell, who not only ruthlessly fought Americans in the Revolution but also survived to antagonize settlers during the War of 1812. Caldwell eventually lived among the Mohawk people and died peacefully in Upper Canada.

As mentioned before, John Carradine was not always a villain. One of his most memorable roles was in the John Steinbeck adaptation of the Pulitzer Prize-winning novel **The Grapes of Wrath**. The story is a gripping tale of the Joad family, who endures the Midwest drought and Great Depression of the early thirties and then decides to travel to become migrant farmers out West. Carradine is a down-and-out preacher named Casey that first

Grapes Of Wrath Headline *(trailer)*

unites the family and then encourages them to make the grueling trek to California. This is his calling. Casey dies trying to unionize the migrant farmers but not without convincing the protagonist, Tom Joad (played by Henry Fonda), that social reform should be the preacher's legacy.

Farmers Migrating to California *(circa 1935)*

The U.S. Census projects that 75 percent of Oklahoma natives toughed out the Midwest drought and stayed on their farms. Steinbeck's novel romanticized a large migration to California. That being said, this might be John Carradine's finest hour in film.

The 1940's were a busy time for Carradine. He co-starred in biographies that included **Brigham Young**, the nineteenth century pioneer that assumed the leadership of the Mormon Church, the adventure movie about the colorful pirate **Captain Kidd,** and the motion picture **Bluebeard** (the modern-day Jack the Ripper that terrorized women in France).

Brigham Young

In **The Adventures of Mark Twain**, Carradine plays rival author, Bret Harte, now barely remembered for his tales of pioneering life in early California. The musical **Paint Your Wagon** is loosely based on one of his writings. Harte was an admirer of Charles Dickens, eulogizing the author with a poem after he died. On the other hand, Mark Twain found Harte to be a phony.

None of these movies were particularly important, except that John Carradine displayed a fondness for playing in the bio-picture genre. In *Of Human Hearts*, he stepped out of the shadows to play President Lincoln during the days that led to the Civil War. However, even this portrayal is incidental to the storyline.

Bret Harte's "M'Liss" *(lithograph)*

The concept of creationism is the Christian alternative to Charles Darwin's theories of evolution. The Bible emerges as an essential book in households of those who believe that God is our Creator. John Carradine appeared in the Old Testament epic *The Ten Commandments*

Aaron and The Golden Calf *(painting)*

as Aaron, the brother of Moses. Aaron in The Bible is the spokesperson for the Hebrews that chose exodus over slavery. Carradine's portrayal is eloquent and persuasive as minister of the Jews. Unfortunately, Aaron allows a golden calf to be created and worshipped while Moses is on his mission to receive the Commandments. In the Book of Deuteronomy, Aaron is spared from the plague because of the intercession of his brother. The Book of Leviticus chronicles the events that eventually lead the noble Aaron to the High Priesthood. Like Moses, Aaron never lived to see the conclusion of their pilgrimage. And so it is written…

Wright Brothers at Kitty Hawk

Jules Verne is the nineteenth century French author who can be considered the Nostradamus of science fiction. Many of his books chronicle the inventive journey of man that has come to pass in the twentieth century. His imaginative novels foresaw the development of the submarine, the archeological discovery of the dinosaur, space travel, and our eventual moon exploration. This visionary lived only to just beyond the turn of the century. But, how gratifying must it have been for Verne to know that the Wright Brothers had actually conquered flight, as he had predicted. ***Around the World in Eighty Days*** is a star-studded adaptation of a Verne novel that was the Best Picture of 1956. The film is set in 1872 England, where the main character, Phileas Fogg (played by the urbane David Niven), makes a wager that he can travel around the world in a set time. Fogg even foretells the eventual ability for man to globe-trot in eighty hours. Today's astronauts and space shuttle inhabitants can attest to this eventual fact. John Carradine is featured in a cameo role while Fogg and his entourage enter the U.S. His

Jules Verne
(French dine novel)

character is Col. Proctor; a poker-playing, loud-mouthed rascal of a man that supports a candidate for high office in bawdy San Francisco. One suspects that this spirited "sidewinder of the West" disappeared after the great earthquake of 1906. Fogg generalizes that all "former

Jules Verne's Autograph

subjects of the Crown" are without morals or manners based on this initial encounter. Proctor is a broad representation of 1870's Americana with humorous undertones. Eventually, Phileas Fogg wins his bet. Jules Verne is the first great writer of the science fiction genre that includes H.G. Wells, Ray Bradbury, and others. In 2008, the government of France initiated efforts to have his remains buried in the Pantheon, alongside other literary giants.

John Ford is considered the finest director of Western film. His last important work was ***The Man Who Shot Liberty Valence***. It is the only movie in which John Wayne and James Stewart appear together. This movie pokes fun at Westerns and the tall tales that they tell. A character in the picture sums up the historical implication of the Old West by boldly stating, "When legend becomes fact, print the legend!" John Carradine is in familiar territory here, playing the fictional advocate of a losing candidate for the Senate. His pomposity is matched only by his verbosity. In retrospect, this was Carradine's last important role, though he made more films after this classic.

John Carradine's work left him in the cracks of biographic cinema. In reality, Carradine was the father of a modern film dynasty. Four of his five sons have

John Carradine/The Hurricane *(trailer)*

gone on to become actors. One son, Keith, won an Academy Award for writing the song "I'm Easy" for the film, ***Nashville.*** We all owe John Carradine a debt of gratitude for connecting the dots to our own American history.

CHAPTER EIGHT

A VOICE FOR BLUE-COLLAR AMERICA

William Bendix (1906-1964)

NO ONE IN HOLLYWOOD'S STUDIO ERA PERSONIFIED LIFE in the urban jungle better than William Bendix. He was the everyman who served, fought, worked, and lived in the trenches of life. More often than not, he is still appreciated for his memorable roles. He could be silly, dumb, amiable, heroic, or menacing...and Bendix lived the *Life of Riley* for his efforts. When needed, he could also pack an award-worthy performance into the mix.

A New York native, Bendix began his adolescence in the limelight as the "bat boy" for the Yankees and was befriended by Babe Ruth, who loved kids. Working as a real-life grocer during the Depression, Bendix found the energy and drive to embark on an improbable chance at a career as an actor.

Babe Ruth
(on and off the field)

Bendix landed his first part in the 1942 film ***Woman of the Year***, which made movie history with the genial pairing of Spencer Tracy and Katharine Hepburn. Tracy and Hepburn went on to make nine films together and are regarded as the screen's most successful couple.

Guadalcanal Campaign

Starting his career during World War II gave Bendix a chance to appear in fine patriotic dramas. ***Wake Island*** is a largely fictional account of the gallantry of soldiers that fought on islands throughout the South Pacific. Paired with Robert Preston, Bendix excelled in the role and earned a Supporting Actor nomination. He also co-starred in ***The Guadalcanal Diary***, which recounts the Marine invasion against the Japanese. What's amazing is the actual battle occurred only a year before the release of the picture. ***Submarine Command*** is a 1950s World War II motion picture that stars William Holden and features Bendix as a member of his crew

Alfred Hitchcock

The 1944 production of ***Lifeboat*** was directed by Alfred Hitchcock and is noted for its talented ensemble cast that featured Tallulah Bankhead, John Hodiak, Walter Slezak, Hume Cronyn, and Bendix. He is convincing as an injured German-American aboard a lifeboat after his ship and U-boat sink from a collision. He dies in the movie and is quite dramatic in the role. Hitchcock always made a cameo in his films, and in this particular movie he appears in a newspaper advertisement; a particularly creative way to be seen.

Though nominated as a Best Supporting Actor in **Wake Island**, the most important film William Bendix appeared in about World War II is the Pulitzer Prize-winning adapted story, **A Bell for Adano**. The story is based on the real life tale of U.S. Army Major Frank Toscani who is placed in charge of Licato, Sicily (*Adano* in the movie), after the Allied invasion. Some of the actions Toscani initiates are free fishing privileges, the use of their mule carts (essential for commerce on the island), and the acquisition of a bell from the Navy to replace the town bell melted down by fascists earlier in the war. Toscani eventually is forced to step down from his command for disobeying a superior officer. The story is a tender endorsement of democratic principles and the liberation of a people.

In lighter moments, Bendix could be the "patsy" or foil for such stars as Abbott and Costello, Bob Hope, and Groucho Marx. Playing a straight man has a history in American cinema that goes back to the silent era. Oliver Hardy, Zeppo Marx, Margaret Dumont, Larry Fine (of *The Three Stooges*), Bing Crosby, and Dean Martin were all adept in the concept of "playing straight" to their counterparts. Bud Abbott was the undisputed "king of the straight men." Bendix showed his comedic skill in low budget comedies that would later serve him well in radio and television.

Film noir was popular in the forties and reached its peak with the release of **Double Indemnity**. Dark, downbeat stories claim the heart of a classic *noir* picture. Usually the characters are uneducated, tough, alienated, and corruptible—whether one was a detective, private investigator, nightclub manager, or gangster. Raymond Chandler was regarded the best in the business as the writer of "private-eye" stories that could be adapted in the *noir* style. His most popular protagonist was Phillip Marlowe. Dashiell Hammett was also known to dabble in *noir*. Hammett's adapted story of **The Glass Key** is an early representation and made Alan Ladd a star. This is William Bendix's most menacing role, and in one particular brutal scene, he beats the Ladd character to a pulp. Bendix is the clear villain in this movie, playing a thug with little regard for life. *The Blue Dahlia* is classic Raymond Chandler *film noir* that includes infidelity, murder, a suspect that is innocent, and

William Bendix/The Dark Corner *(trailer)*

the dark streets of an unnamed city, which adds to the mystery of the plot. Bendix appears as Ladd's loyal buddy back home from the war. He also appeared in **The Dark Corner**, which starred Lucille Ball in a rare dramatic turn; and **The Web** in which Bendix actually plays an unsympathetic cop who investigates (what else) a killing. His last

Playwright Eugene O'Neill

noir pictures were 1949's **The Big Steal**, starring another veteran of the genre, Robert Mitchum, and **Cover Up**, again playing a sheriff. William Bendix was a reliable co-star in *film noir,* which incidentally, worked well in movies that were produced in rich black and white.

Every once in a while, a worthy script from an important writer would be laid at the doorstep of Bendix, right next to "the morning newspaper and empty milk bottles." The great laureate in literature, Eugene O'Neill was the first American playwright to introduce realism into his work, learning his technique from Anton Chekov, a Russian, and Henrik Ibsen, a Swede. Many of his characters live in the fringe of society and have their hopes for a better life ultimately dashed by the needs of their superiors. O'Neill's best work includes *Mourning Becomes Electra*, *The Iceman Cometh*, and *Long Day's Journey into Night*, and

Writer William Saroyan

started the expressionist period of literature in the early half of the twentieth century. He inspired the writings of Tennessee Williams and Arthur Miller. After his death, his home in Northern California was preserved as a historical site in 1976. His acclaimed play *The Hairy Ape* was adapted into a movie in 1944 and features Bendix as a laborer known as "Yank." One day, a rich daughter of an industrialist calls him "a filthy beast." He wanders the streets of New York unable to find his identity, a member of the work force alienated by a capitalist system that enjoys the persecution and dehumanization of the working class. The oppression of the human condition by the societal world of the privileged is a common theme in many of O'Neill's plays.

On the other side of the coin, William Bendix is quite solid in the movie based on William Saroyan's Pulitzer Prize-winning play *The Time of Your Life*. The film depicts optimism in the face of despair, a slice-of-life look at a waterfront saloon set in San Francisco.

Babe Ruth and President Warren Harding

Shoeless Joe Jackson

Bendix plays the barkeep that is visited by an assortment of colorful types, and the film stars James Cagney as a patron. The television program **Cheers** captures many of its core ideas from this lively portrait of folks who live for "a bit of the bubbly." This is Bendix at his definitive best.

William Bendix fulfilled a lifelong dream to play his idol in *The Babe Ruth Story*. It's a fictionalized account about the exploits of the popular New York Yankee player that saved baseball after the Black Sox Scandal of 1919. The Chicago White Sox team was accused of throwing games during that year's World Series, and several members of the club (including potential Hall of Famer "Shoeless" Joe Jackson) were permanently expelled from the game. "The Babe" personified the Roaring Twenties, from his uncanny ability to hit home runs to his off-the-field antics. When one reporter asked Ruth why he made more money than the president, he replied, "Well, I had a better year!"

President Harding *(editorial cartoon)*

Bendix captured the fun-loving nature of this larger-than-life Paul Bunyan-esque ball player.

The Connecticut Yankee in King Arthur's Court is a film based on a story written by Mark Twain, and it gave Bendix a rare opportunity to sing and dance with Bing Crosby. This fantasy was one of the most enjoyed movies of 1949.

Throughout the 1950s, Bendix appeared in a wide range of movies including **Detective Story**, **Blackbeard, the Pirate**, and **Macao.** He is also one of the many screen actors that brought his talent to radio, the essential entertainment source in homes prior to the advent of television.

Crime drama and science fiction were popular genres in radio. In fact, the whole nation was overcome by hysteria when Orson Welles produced ***The War of the Worlds*** in October of 1938. Many Americans actually believed that Martians invaded parts of the Northeast. Welles credited his team of players and the gifted writings of H. G. Wells for the effective radio prank.

The situation comedy also has its roots in radio during Hollywood's Golden Age. Shows such as **Fibber McGee and Molly**, **The Jack Benny Program**, and **Edgar Bergen and Charlie McCarthy** were popular programs of the thirties and forties. The most listened-to program was **Amos 'n' Andy**, heard by a third of the U.S. at its peak. By today's standards, **Amos 'n' Andy** is a politically incorrect view of the lives of urban blacks of the period, portrayed by two white performers. However its stars, Charles Correll and Freeman Gos-

War Of The Worlds *(circa 1906 drawing)*

den took enormous measures to portray these stereotypes as caring family men and contributors to society.

It was in this atmosphere that **The Life of Riley** was created. Bendix is best known for playing the lovable, dim-witted family man, Chester A. Riley. *Riley* accomplished for Bendix on radio what **I Love Lucy** did for Lucille Ball on television; it made him a household name. The everyman lived in the big city, and his antics were quite relatable. "What a revoltin' development this is" entered the lexicon of American culture. Riley was the prototype of the blue-collar guy that was often imitated in television comedy, beginning with Ralph Kramden in **The Honeymooners** and the animated Fred Flintstone. Other popular characters that were created as homage to *Riley:* Archie Bunker, Dan Conner (the husband of **Roseanne**), and Doug Hefferman (**The King of Queens**). Bendix also appeared as Riley in movies and had his own television show that ran until 1958. The program went into reruns but disappeared after Bendix died in 1964.

William Bendix excelled in all mediums of entertainment. He spoke in popular American vernacular about the trials and tribulations of average folks. He's still a part of our society that exists today, and his exploits should never be forgotten as long as we have air to breathe.

William Bendix/Macao *(trailer)*

CHAPTER NINE

HOLLYWOOD'S PATRIARCH

Donald Crisp (1882-1974)

ONE OF HOLLYWOOD'S PIONEERS, the English-born Donald Crisp appeared in and directed movies as far back as 1908. Renowned playwright and composer George M. Cohan was Crisp's protégé when he first arrived in the U.S. in 1906. He became acquainted with movie director D. W. Griffith, and they both traveled to Hollywood in 1912. Griffith is credited with creating the motion picture narrative in long form (over sixty minutes) with his landmark production of **The Birth of a Nation** in 1915. Crisp had appeared in bit parts in short films up until then, when not directing.

Director D.W. Griffith *(postage stamp)*

The Birth of a Nation secured the future of full-length feature films, and for that alone, the movie is considered culturally significant. It was quite popular at the time of its release, grossing more than ten million dollars and was required viewing at President Woodrow Wilson's

White House. The movie chronicles pre-Civil War America, travels through the battle between the North and South, and endures Reconstruction and the unfortunate practice of carpetbagging (Northern politicos victoriously claiming land as their own in the beleagured South).

The problem with the film lies in the script, which portrays Negroes as renegades and paints a sympathetic portrait in the rise of the Ku Klux Klan. Even worse, African American characters were played by white actors painted in blackface. This was a common practice in the early part of the twentieth century, especially in minstrel shows and vaudeville (noted performers Al Jolson and Eddie Cantor would do routines in blackface). The Klan in the movie restores the South's stability by eliminating voter fraud that empowers Southern blacks and successfully ends Reconstruction. The Northern protaganist in the motion picture is based on real-life Congressman Thaddeus Stevens. The Ku Klux Klan used the movie for many decades as a recruitment piece, pointing to the lynching that occurs in the film as a necessary evil. The National Association for the Advancement of Colored People (NAACP, founded in 1909) and black historians, including W. E. B. Du Bois, universally condemned the picture as fabrication and rascist in the portrayal of the Negro, who were actually fighting for the elimination of slaveryand their freedom. President Wilson believed it as an

Rep. Thadeus Stevens

unfortunately true depiction of the period. To appease the protesters, D. W. Griffith would produce ***Intolerance*** as his creative apology. Donald Crisp is General Ulysses S. Grant in the motion picture.

Crisp had a long career playing patriarchs in American families. His first important screen-father was in the silent film ***Broken Blossoms***. The movie was made in 1919 and starred Lillian Gish. In the picture, Crisp's character is brutal and abusive, a far cry from future roles.

With the advent of "talkies" (motion pictures with dialogue), Donald Crisp would embark on a thirty-year career in supporting parts. The 1930s was a busy time for the actor, appearing in *Mutiny on the Bounty*, *The Charge of the Light Brigade*, *Mary of Scotland*, *The Life of Emile Zola*, *The Dawn Patrol*, *Juarez*, *Wuthering Heights*, *The Sea Hawk*, and *The Private Lives of Elizabeth and Essex*. Crisp was comfortable playing in period pieces that primarily told European (and particularly British) stories based in fact.

W. E. B. DuBois

A notable exception in this period was *Jezebel* in 1938, which takes place around the Battle of Antebellum during the Civil War. Crisp is a doctor in the movie, fighting yellow fever, a common infirmity during the war. Sometimes called the "American plague," the disease was actually more prevalent prior to the Civil War in Norfolk and New Orleans and in the 1870s in Memphis. A research paper by Walter Reed in 1900 led to a U.S government program in 1905 to educate folks about the source of the disease. Dr. Reed credits Cuban physician, Carlos Finlay, in determining that yellow fever was transmitted by mosquitoes. Due to Reed's efforts, the Panama Canal could be completed. A vaccine that provides a semblance of immunity was subsequently developed in 1937, though

Dr. Walter Reed

no actual cure exists. *Jezebel* was Warner Bros.' response to the impending release of MGM's **Gone with the Wind**.

With war on the horizon, motion pictures of the early 1940s would begin to focus on stories with American themes. Crisp would adapt

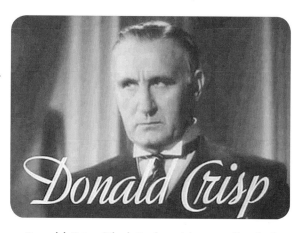

Donald Crisp/That Certain Woman *(trailer)*

by concentrating on paternal roles. He was so successful that he was typecast as the prototypical patriarch during the rest of his career. His first significant film was **Knute Rockne, All American**. Pat O'Brien

Notre Dame Coach Knute Rockne

plays Notre Dame's flamboyant coach, and Ronald Reagan co-stars as one of his students, George Gipp. Crisp is Father John Callahan, an Irish priest and mentor to Rockne during his successful career at the University. "Win one for the Gipper" is the immortal line uttered by George Gipp before he dies in the movie. Knute Rockne compiled a record of 105 victories and six national championships during his tenure at Notre Dame. He died in a 1931 plane crash and was only forty-three years of age.

Donald Crisp appeared in the fourth screen adaptation of Robert Louis Stevenson's

Dr. Jekyll and Mr. Hyde. Crisp's character is murdered by Mr. Hyde without ever learning that his daughter's engagement to Dr. Jekyll is doomed because of his scientific tampering with nature. Superior versions of the novella were produced in 1920 and 1931. Regarded in his time as an essayist and writer, Stevenson's printed words in the nineteenth century were translated by more countries than the works of Charles Dickens, Edgar Allen Poe, and Oscar Wilde. Today, he has been relegated as the forerunner to the horror-film genre and is not considered a relevant author.

How Green Was My Valley was the important film of 1941. In many ways, the movie is considered to be John Ford's finest and was voted the Best Picture over such great films as ***Citizen Kane***, ***The Maltese Falcon***, ***Suspicion***, and ***Seargent York***. This is the motion picture that defined Donald Crisp as an actor. He is the head of a turn-of-the-century Welsh mining family. His character, Gwilym Morgan, displays honesty, integrity, and a stern disposition as the father of six boys and one girl. He dies at the end of the film as a result of a mining accident. This was the only time that Donald Crisp was nominated for Supporting Actor, and he won the statuette.

Crisp didn't mind taking a back seat to the most popular star of the forties, a collie named Lassie. With the help of this intelligent dog, he would teach valuable life lessons to his son, played by Roddy McDowall (who was his youngest in *Valley*). ***Lassie Come Home*** was the first in the series that culminated in additional movies, radio, and eventually, television. Crisp would go on to play opposite the legendary collie in four films. Lassie was actually named Pal and owned and trained

A Collie *(drawing resembling Lassie)*

by Rudd Weatherwax, who would obtain the trademark to the name. Crisp also appeared in other canine classics including, *A Dog of Flanders* and *Greyfriars Bobby: The Story of a Dog*.

Crisp co-starred in *National Velvet* as father to Elizabeth Taylor. This is a heartwarming story about a young girl's quest to become a Grand National Steeplechase champion in Sussex, England. This is vintage Crisp in his advisory capacity as the paternal symbol of common sense, decency, and warmth.

Every once in a while, Donald Crisp would play a villain. In *Bright Leaf*, he is a rival to Gary Cooper. The story is loosely based on post-Civil War tobacco tycoons, Washington Duke and George McElwee. The film vilifies the carpetbagging tendencies of the Crisp character.

In *The Man from Laramie*, Crisp is the honorable if jaded father of two boys rivaling for his attention. The movie is based in part on William Shakespeare's *King Lear*, with Crisp as a Western baron. In the play, Lear divides his realm among three daughters, with the one showing the most affection receiving the largest share of the estate. The competition causes Lear to go insane, and he eventually dies from the ordeal. In *Laramie*, Alec Waggoman (the Crisp role) goes blind (in a fitting tribute to Lear's madness) and is critically injured by one of his sons (played by Arthur Kennedy). He realizes that both have gone astray in their search for his father's affection. Waggoman's metaphoric blindness has all but destroyed his family. Shakespeare transplants well in a Western setting.

King Lear/First Edition *(title page)*

Grand Tetons

In his sixth decade in motion pictures, Donald Crisp was at home in family drama. He appears as a mayor in Disney's **Pollyanna**. His last film role in **Spencer's Mountain** earned him the well-deserved title of "Grandpa" Spencer. The movie takes place in and around the Grand Tetons in Wyoming. Henry Fonda stars in the picture, which became the basis for the popular television drama, *The Waltons*. The Emmy-winning series, in many ways, is a lasting tribute to the kind of movies Donald Crisp is best remembered for.

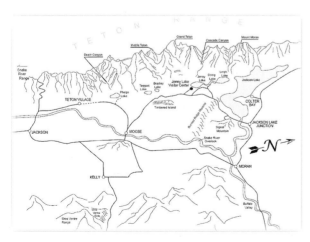

Teton Range *(area map)*

His career began with the advent of the motion picture

as a premier narrative source of information and entertainment. He is in some of the first work ever put on film. His contribution makes him an elder of Hollywood's elite, and he stands alone as the best example in our struggle to create ideal family values. For these reasons, Donald Crisp should be considered "the father of modern American cinema."

Donald Crisp/City For Conquest (trailer)

CHAPTER TEN

CHAIRMAN OF THE BOARD

Van Heflin (1908-1971)

AUTHORITY IS A PERVASIVE CONCEPT that embraces our American history. Its origins lie in tandem with organization as Eastern cities began to industrialize and Western territories grew into cities and states. Hard-working ranchers and farmers would get elected as town elders in small outposts, and the law would replace frontier justice. Obedience in the military could lead to success through the ranks. Folks up to the challenge would build our country from the ground up. Eventually, modern progress was measured in profits, and

War Production Board *(1942)*

a person's worth, by promotions and bonuses. When Hollywood eventually wanted its actor in a suit and tie to star in a movie, William Holden would get the call. When the movies had smaller budgets, or a supporting player was needed, Van Heflin was your guy.

Heflin alternated throughout his career in supporting and starring roles, always the sensible, serious, and sometimes brooding character in the motion picture. Corporate America is filled with many types, and Heflin could play them all. Even in historical films, he displayed great intelligence. Van Heflin wasn't always the hero, but he was a dependable ally in making the movie believable and compelling. He never received a bad review, even if the picture was a real "stinker." At the time, his peers referred to Heflin as an "actor's actor." The story of Van Heflin coincides with the rise of our business acumen that is still paying dividends every time we watch his performances.

He made his screen debut in the Victorian period piece, *A Woman Rebels*. Katharine Hepburn is an enlightened woman who defies her autocratic father by bearing a child out of wedlock and eventually establishing herself as a journalist. Heflin plays her suitor; though feminism is at the heart of the film. He would later co-star with Hepburn on Broadway in *The Philadelphia Story* in the role made famous by James Stewart in the movie adaptation.

An early chance for Heflin to show his ease at portraying executive-types came to him in *H. M. Pulham, Esq.*, produced in 1941. He plays a gentleman in advertising that helps his friend (the Robert Young character) get a job. The film suggests that he is a Harvard graduate who is no stranger to success. This small picture would have a huge impact in the casting of Heflin in future films.

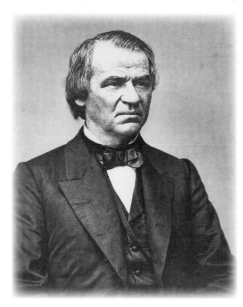

President Andrew Johnson

Early in Heflin's career, he showed great promise in historic stories. In *Tennessee Johnson*, he portrays the man who would actually become our seventeenth President, who rises from his humble beginnings as a tailor in becoming governor, U.S.

Senator, and eventually, vice president. Fate intercedes as Lincoln is assassinated, and Johnson inherits the presidency. He applies the policy of Reconstruction to the war-torn South. The policy is a disaster, and he is impeached for his efforts. The movie paints this beleagured president as a simple, plain-spoken hero. In truth, Johnson was a hot-headed Southern Democrat that supported the North during the Civil War. As president, he vetoed twenty-nine bills passed through Congress; a presidential record at the time. Congress overturned fifteen of those vetoes (also a record). He was a man that was reviled by the South as a traitor and as Lincoln's unpopular successor in the North.

Johnson's Impeachment Papers
(editorial cartoon)

Three Musketeers and D'Artagnan
(drawing)

The Three Musketeers was one of the great novels by French author, Alexandre Dumas, who also wrote **The Count of Monte Cristo** and **The Man in the Iron Mask**. His stories were gallant tales that were read by the entire world. His books have inspired over two hundred movies. In the 1948 adaption, D'Artagnan is the Gascon youth that aspires to join the Musketeers. The epic adventure features Gene

Kelly as D'Artagnan, and Heflin plays Athos, the Musketeer that frankly finds D'Artagnan a bit of a nuisance. This rousing motion picture also stars Lana Turner, June Allyson, Frank Morgan, Angela Lansbury, and Vincent Price as the evil Cardinal Richelieu. Heflin is heroic and ill tempered in this rather amusing role as the King's Musketeer. Alexandre Dumas is buried in the Pantheon with other great French writers.

During World War II, Heflin was a commissioned navel officer and, while he served, lent his voice to a number of military documentaries including *Screen Snapshots: Hollywood in Uniform, Land and Live in the Jungle*, and *Land and Live in the Desert*. After the war, he joined Robert Montgomery and Robert Taylor to narrate *The Secret Land*, an award-winning documentary that chronicled the 1946 Antarctic expedition of polar explorer, Lt. Com. Richard Byrd. Actual color footage is used, and the film cemented Byrd's modern hero status.

Athos/King's Musketeer
(lithograph)

Lt. Com. Richard E. Byrd

Van Heflin would win the Best Supporting Actor award of 1942 for his portrayal of a loyal drunken friend in the crime film *Johnny Eager*. His acting depth was obvious and MGM was eager to utilize the versatile actor, but the studio would have to wait until he completed his military service.

Returning from the war, Heflin would appear in a series of melodramas. **The Strange Love of Martha Ivers** is a *film noir* story that starred Barbara Stanwyck and Kirk Douglas (in his screen debut). Heflin plays a noble drifter that gets caught up in

Van Heflin/Grand Central Murder *(trailer)*

a love-triangle. His fortune is not so good in his next role. **Possessed** features Joan Crawford as a *femme fatale*, and Heflin her inevitable victim. This movie gives him the chance to play an engineer, an otherwise normal character that is doomed by Crawford's obsessive behavior.

Heflin would shine in intelligent Westerns of the 1950s. **Shane** is the definitive classic that stars Alan Ladd and Jean Arthur. Brandon DeWilde is memorable as Heflin's son who idolizes Shane. Shane is part and parcel a representative of the lawless West, with gunfights as the only way to settle disputes. In contrast, Heflin's role represents the future of civilized communities, where law and order must thrive for a town to grow and prosper. Heflin steals the film as the conflicted father who wants to be brave for his son. He is also the responsible homesteader who understands the nature of walking away from a fight, especially when the chips are stacked against you. Ultimately, Shane rids the town of the murderous gunslingers. He then leaves, allowing a father to teach his son lessons of what real bravery is about.

3:10 to Yuma is another smart Western that stars Glenn Ford as a rare villain, and Van Heflin. Again, Heflin displays integrity as the family man who witnesses a stagecoach holdup. His simple task is to put the Glenn Ford character on a train (now a captured prisoner). Standing in the way is Ford's gang of outlaws, hell-bent on freeing their friend. Ford's character is a study in redemption as he grows to appreciate the valiant if foolhardy effort by Heflin. The actors play well together in this popular film.

Pancho Villa Expedition *(circa 1916)*

Other Westerns that would feature Heflin include *They Came to Cordura*, a fictionalized account that takes place during the 1916 U.S. expedition into Mexico to capture Pancho Villa— a real trek made by General John J. Pershing and his troops; and a remake of **Stagecoach**, which he plays the U.S Marshall set on safely delivering the passengers across the frontier. John Ford's version of the film is superior.

The corporate drama came into prominence during the 1950s. *Executive Suite* was the best example of the genre and starred William Holden, Barbara Stanwyck, and Fredric March. Other fine films that exemplify authority and business storylines include **12 Angry Men** and **The Apartment.** However, the actor that is the personification of the modern corporate film is Van Heflin. **Woman's World** is a motion picture with an ensemble cast of talented players that include Lauren Bacall, Fred MacMurray, June Allyson, Cornell Wilde, Arlene Dahl, and of course, Heflin. The wily Clifton Webb must decide among three candidates who should replace the general manager of a motor company. This movie captures the spirit of executive competition and the eternal battle for normalcy at home.

Patterns is a significant 1955 piece that was written by the up-and-coming Rod Serling. Today, Serling is remembered as the creator of **The Twilight Zone**. However in the fifties, the writer wrote some of the best scripts in television. He was a constant contributor for many of the anthology programs that were popular at the time, including **Playhouse 90, Suspense, Studio One, Hallmark Hall of Fame**, and **Kraft Television Theatre**. The teleplays, **Requiem for a Heavyweight**,

Seven Days in May, and *Patterns*, were adapted to the big screen. *Patterns* is the dynamic drama about the relationship between a boss and his subordinates in business. The boardroom serves as a compelling stage for the story of a rising corporate star and his empathy for the partner he is destined to replace. Everett Sloane, Ed Begley, and Richard Kiley starred in the teleplay. When it became a big screen picture, Heflin replaced Kiley. Rod Serling won the first of his six Emmys for this acclaimed portrait of white-collar life.

A return to Broadway provided Van Heflin a chance to appear in superior productions of Arthur Miller stories. He valued the opportunity in working with Miller, and like Arthur Kennedy, Heflin would provide complex characterizations in *A Memory of Two Mondays* and *A View from the Bridge*.

In 1963, Van Heflin made a war movie called *Cry of Battle*. The film is about a fictional campaign in the Philippines during World War II. The picture itself isn't particularly important. Its significance is that it was the featured film at the movie theatre in the Dallas suburb where Lee Harvey Oswald hid the day he shot President Kennedy. He was arrested at this location. To document this historic event, "Lee Harvey Oswald, November 22, 1963" was later painted on the chair he occupied (the fifth seat from the aisle in the third to last row).

Ironically, Heflin's final film would give the actor a chance to play

Lee Harvey Oswald *(mugshots)*   Dallas Theatre *(site of Oswald arrest)*

a business failure. As D. O. Guerrero in *Airport*, he decides that the only way to make his way out of mounting debt is to blow up a plane, so his wife can collect the insurance. His despair is obvious. When he fails at making the disaster look like an accident, he sets off the bomb that proves to be his legacy. Guerrero and his wife (played by Maureen Stapleton) are the models of the fleeting nature of "what might have been." It's easy to empathize with the couple, at the risk of rooting for the obvious villain in the motion picture. *Airport* was the first in the disaster-film genre that became popular throughout the seventies.

Van Heflin achieved a certain measure of stardom, and today's film fans might remember him better had he not prematurely died of a heart attack. His career was relatively brief but incredibly memorable because he was so natural on screen. He paved the way for today's actors in their search for realism in characters. His modern dramas were not always the biggest films at the time (except for *Shane* and *Airport*), but the avid film fan could do a lot worse than spend a few hours with Van Heflin.

Van Heflin/Possessed *(trailer)*

CHAPTER ELEVEN

A TOE IN THE WATER

Eddie "Rochester" Anderson
(1905-1977)

HOLLYWOOD OF THE THIRTIES, FORTIES, AND FIFTIES spent much of its collective energy trying to mirror society. Movies were made that captured an American spirit that fought hard against the Great Depression and global dictators that forced us into another World War. The unfortunate truth is that movie studios of the era didn't understand or had little regard for the social ills that date as far back as the origins of this country. Our founding fathers compromised on some areas of concern, which eventually led us into the Civil War. It's not surprising that other factions of society couldn't face delicate social issues either. The largest of these problems was a racism that is still prevalent in some corners of our country. Historically, the issue of race relations has always needed to be addressed.

Pancho Villa

In the entertainment industry, a certain measure of defiance was essential to fight the good fight. The first round in this battle was the tearing down of stereotypes. From a movie studio's point of view, it was too easy to paint with a broad brush the face of an entire people. When Wallace Beery played Pancho Villa, Hispanics were cast in big sombreros, with bullets across their chest, and with heavy accents. Arabs were portrayed as camel riders, belly dancers, and turban-wearing villains. Worst of all, blacks were regarded as lazy-talking, foot-shuffling, ignorant people and the butt of humor and ridicule. The sad fact is that some actors of color had to go along with these false associations to put food on their family's table.

This chapter is not about those folks that kept stereotypes in place. Black and white folks had plenty of reasons for allowing this indignity to occur for so long. I choose to highlight individuals who paved the way for race to be incidental in scripts, entertainment, and in life. For example, the Screen Actor's Guild (SAG) reports that the first African American to join an acting union was Noble Johnson. He received his SAG card in 1933.

Paul Robeson (*profile drawing*)

One of the most eloquent gatecrashers of "Jim Crow" America was Paul Robeson. His father was a slave in North Carolina who managed to find his way to Pennsylvania, where he graduated from Lincoln University and became a successful minister. Paul grew up in a climate of education and creative application. He was only the third African American to be accepted to Rutgers University, and he excelled in athletics, singing, acting, and of course, academics. Robeson graduated Phi Beta Kappa and was his class valedictorian. He later graduated from Columbia Law School.

Paul Robeson would have been a fine lawyer had he not found early fame as a vocalist and actor. A true bass singer, Robeson embarked on a radio career during the 1920s. He traveled to England to perform Shakespeare at a time when no American stage company would hire him. It wasn't until 1945 that the U.S. allowed Robeson to star in **Othello**. As of 2009, the show still holds the record for the longest running Shakespearean play on Broadway.

Paul Robeson/Othello

His most famous role was as Joe, first in the 1928 London production of **Showboat** and eventually on Broadway. Film audiences marveled at his performance of Ole Man River in 1936. His Hollywood career is brief, but important. He took on assignments that told the tales of his ancestral predecessors and approached his oversimplified roles with dignity and passion.

Paul Robeson's personal story is more significant. He addressed owners of major league baseball as early as 1943 to integrate the game. In 1946, he founded the American Crusade against Lynching (among the members was Albert Einstein). Unfortunately, the FBI investigated his activities for almost thirty years. In 1950, the State Department denied Robeson a passport to keep him out of Russia. In 1956, speaking before the House Un-American Activities Committee, Robeson pointed out the hypocrisy of their fight against Communism, while virtually ignoring the rights of minorities that led to segregation in schools, voting impropriety, and other "Jim Crow" laws. He lived long enough to witness the enactment of the Voting Rights Bill in 1965 and his name eventually associated with civil liberties for all persons of color.

The House of Representatives held a memorial after his death in 1976, the first in a long line of accolades for this champion of justice. *Paul Robeson: Tribute to an Artist* won an Academy Award in 1980 for Best Documentary Short Subject. In 1995, he was inducted into the College Football Hall of Fame. *Turner Classic Movies* proudly started airing his movies, which effectively lifted the ban of his films in the U.S.

Marian Anderson

Marian Anderson was the best opera singer of her generation. As with most youngsters of devout parents, she began singing in her church and was adept in singing mainstream gospel music. Her big break came as a result of taking first prize in a singing competition sponsored by the New York Philharmonic. She eventually performed at Carnegie Hall. Brought up in Philadelphia, she wasn't subject to as much racism as was common in other parts of the country. However, she was denied entry to the Philadelphia Music Academy because she was "colored." Anderson didn't necessarily see herself as a champion for civil rights. However, her extraordinary talent put her in the cross hair of the movement.

In 1939, Eleanor Roosevelt invited Anderson to perform for a Daughter's of the American Revolution recital that was set up at Constitution Hall. The D.A.R. denied permission for her to sing (to a mostly integrated audience), and Roosevelt promptly resigned from the organization. Mrs. Roosevelt and Walter White (Executive Secretary of the NAACP) persuaded Secretary of the Interior Harold Ickes to arrange an open-air concert at the steps of the Lincoln Memorial.

Seventy-five hundred people attended the concert. Radio stations broadcasted the event, which made Anderson an international star. She eventually sang at Constitution Hall during World War II at a Red Cross benefit.

Eleanor Roosevelt and Marian Anderson

To celebrate the seventieth anniversary of her famed concert, the Abraham Lincoln Bicentennial Commission held a memorial concert where Marian Anderson sang. On April 12, 2009, black opera singer Denyce Graves performed three of the same songs, including "America" and "Ave Maria." The program featured former Secretary of State Colin Powell's reciting of portions of Lincoln's second Inaugural Address. The concert also coincided with Barack Obama's historic inauguration as president.

Secretary Of State Colin Powell

Nat "King" Cole was a celebrated jazz pianist, who also appeared in a few movies. Inspired by the greats of his time including Louis Armstrong, Earl Hines, and Duke Ellington, Cole forged an impressive career. He was also a noted singer and performed one of the most popular holiday pieces of all time: "The Christmas Song." He was one of the first performers that would refuse to do live shows in segregated venues.

Duke Ellington

Eartha Kitt

Cole made history as the first black performer to host a television show. His show aired despite national advertisers refusing to sponsor the program. Many of his contemporaries were invited, and guests including Ella Fitzgerald, Harry Belafonte, and Eartha Kitt. Well-spoken and humble, he was a natural on television. He was also a pioneer in influencing Negroes voting in presidential elections when he supported John Kennedy in 1960. Nat Cole was posthumously given a lifetime Grammy award in 1990.

Which brings us to the most prolific black character actor of the period, Eddie Anderson (known as "Rochester"). Though cast as a servant or butler in most of his roles, he transcended the stereotypes, which were common in movies of the period. He is a true rebel when considering what he was up against. Anderson was a natural comic and gifted actor

```
TELEGRAM              MARCH 11, 1960
BY PHONE:  7:15 p.m.

MR. NAT COLE
401 SO. MUIRFIELD DRIVE
LOS ANGELES, CALIF.

I CERTAINLY APPRECIATE YOUR WILLINGNESS TO HELP ME IN THE
CAMPAIGN HERE IN WISCONSIN.  I WOULD LIKE TO HAVE HAD YOU
WITH ME ON MY VISITS AROUND THE STATE BUT I UNDERSTAND THAT
OUR SCHEDULES PRECLUDE US BEING HERE TOGETHER.  UNDER THESE
CIRCUMSTANCES I WOULD HOPE THAT IN ONE OF THE PRIMARIES THAT
IS TO FOLLOW WISCONSIN THAT YOU WOULD BE WILLING TO ASSIST
ME.  I AM MOST GRATEFUL TO YOU.  BEST REGARDS.

                        JOHN F. KENNEDY


CHARGED TO

ROBERT F. KENNEDY
SCHROEDER HOTEL
ROOM 1624
MILWAUKEE, WIS.
```

Kennedy Telegram
(thanking Nat Cole)

who made over sixty motion pictures. There isn't a person that lived during the era that wouldn't recognize his raspy voice. His first role was in 1932's **What Price Hollywood?**

"Race pictures" were an early alternative to what mainstream Hollywood considered accurate. These were movies that were made by black directors and actors, and they were distributed to movie theatres in African American neighborhoods. Anderson honed his skills in these films. MGM produced **Cabin in the Sky**, which starred an all-black cast, including the popular Ethel Waters, Lena Horne, and Anderson. The characters in the motion picture were richer portraits of black America (though not perfect), which included family and neighborhood life. It was a project by noted Director Vincente Minnelli.

Eddie Anderson appeared in **Jezebel** and **Kentucky** in 1938 and in back-to-back Best Pictures of the 1930s, playing the cook in **You Can't Take It with You** and as Uncle Peter in **Gone with the Wind**. This was a remarkable accomplishment for any actor. His characters rang true as he didn't resort to total generalizations.

His most important contribution to Hollywood would be his long association with a highly visible comic in radio. **The Jack Benny Program** was an immensely popular show that featured Benny as the straight man to a talented ensemble cast of players that included his wife Mary Livingstone, announcer Don Wilson, band leader Phil Harris, and vocalist Dennis Day (among others). In many ways, the funniest member of the cast was Eddie "Rochester" Anderson. His debut in 1937 as Benny's valet was unlike any portrayal of black America that radio audiences had ever heard. He was witty, sarcastic, and intelligent. Anderson always had the opportunity to one-up the star, which he did to perfection. Jack Benny's team of writers understood the sophistication of the listeners. Anderson became the most popular member of the talented ensemble. Benny was very protective of Anderson, and he would refuse to play in theatres or stay in hotels that refused his co-star's fair treatment. This was a profound message sent to Americans by a top comedian who had high regards for his friend. In 1969, Anderson appeared in a Jack Benny television special, joking that no comedy bits would be performed involving "Rochester" as a butler. Eddie Anderson openly wept at Benny's funeral in 1974.

He played "Roches-
ter" in the movies *Topper
Returns* and *Buck Benny
Rides Again*, and in some
of the top radio shows of
the day. In fact, his part
was so big in the 1945
film *Brewster's Millions,*
the picture was actually
banned in some Memphis
and Mississippi theatres.

Eddie Anderson/Topper Returns *(trailer)*

Anderson enjoyed a
cameo role in *It's a Mad
Mad Mad Mad World* in 1963. He plays a taxi driver who joins a
group of citizens looking for buried money that is the essence of greed
in the movie. Anderson holds his own with Ethel Merman, Milton
Berle, and Jonathan Winters, among others in the cast. The cabbie is
even offered "one equal share" of the cash. Kudos to director Stanley
Kramer for this incidental symbolic gesture.

Eddie "Rochester" Anderson set the stage for Sidney Poitier, James

Earl Jones, Paul Winfield, Louis Gos-
sett Jr., and many black actors who
followed in movies; and Richard
Pryor, Eddie Murphy, and others in
contemporary comedy. The Black
Film Makers Hall of Fame honored
him in 1975 with the Oscar Micheaux
Award; and the Radio Hall of Fame
posthumously inducted the comedian
in 2001. His "toe in the water" would
make a splash against racism. Delivering witty characterizations exem-
plified what it meant to stand up for
what is appropriate that served him
well in film, radio, and television. The

Poitier, Belafonte and Heston
at Lincoln Memorial

country is rich for his effort.

CHAPTER TWELVE

LADIES-IN-WAITING

WOMEN HAVE BEEN IMPORTANT IN OUR HISTORY. John Adams had Abigail for advice as Colonials moved towards the Revolution. Betsy Ross sewed our first American flag. Clara Barton started the American Red Cross. Women fought for the right to vote and other reforms for over half a century as part of the Suffrage Movement. World War II had its share of women who served with distinction in the military, and our female civilian population was instrumental in helping build weaponry and equipment that was essential in our war effort.

Betsy Ross House *(display)*

Clara Barton

Female Suffrage Parade *(circa 1914)*

Women during World War II
(editorial cartoon)

Hollywood had legendary actresses during its Golden Age. Yet, important supporting roles for women, especially in historical motion pictures, were scarce. It was hard to write a specific chapter about any one standout for this book. That being said, I found it appealing to look back at several talented supporting actresses that worked diligently to find worthy motion picture projects in the studio era.

Gale Sondergaard, Claire Trevor, Mary Astor, Hattie McDaniel, Jane Darwell, Teresa Wright, Marjorie Main, Agnes Moorhead, Angela Lansbury, and two-time Oscar winner, Shelley Winters, all carved storied careers. They played a variety of roles of contextual importance and interesting characters from literature.

Teresa Wright/Best Years
Of Our Lives *(trailer)*

Let me single out three talented actresses that created consistent personas that defined their purpose...

Gloria Grahame (1923-1981)

Gloria Grahame/Macao
(trailer)

No one performed as the fallen woman better than Gloria Grahame. She was the bad girl with "the heart of gold." Grahame played to type in *It's a Wonderful Life*; *Song of the Thin Man*, the finale in the William Powell/ Myrna Loy series, *In a Lonely Place*, co-starring Humphrey Bogart; and *The Big Heat*, playing a *femme fatale* who is brutally disfigured with scalding hot coffee.

In 1952, she appeared in four popular pictures, including her award-winning performance in *The Bad and the Beautiful*, and in the film chosen as Best Picture that year, Cecil B. DeMille's *The Greatest Show On Earth*. It's an all-star exposé of the circus. The concept of "three ring" entertainment is the brainchild of nineteenth century showman P. T. Barnum.

Ringling Bros. Circus
(circus poster)

Grahame also played Ado Annie, "the girl that can't say no," in the Rogers and Hammerstein adapted Broadway musical *Oklahoma*. In a wide range of roles, Gloria Grahame put on display the "blemishes" of her characterizations.

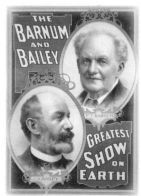

P.T. Barnum
(circus poster)

Beulah Bondi (1888-1981)

Hollywood's matriarch, Beulah Bondi, played moms with warmth and common sense in many of Hollywood's most memorable motion pictures. She played the mother of James Stewart four different times, including *Mr. Smith Goes to Washington* and *It's a Wonderful Life.* Her maternal instincts were on display in the classic films *On Borrowed Time*, *Our Town*, *The Southerner*, *The Snake Pit*, *Remember the Night*, and *The Very Thought of You*.

Rachel Jackson *(portrait)*

In one of her best roles, Bondi portrayed Andrew Jackson's wife, Rachel (who died just before Jackson took office as president), in *The Gorgeous Hussy*. President Jackson blamed gossip initiated by his opponents during the campaigns of 1824 (and 1828) for his loss. *The Age of Jackson* (which stretched through the presidency of James K. Polk) identifies his legacy, which in part attempted to punish his detractors who cost him his beloved Rachel.

Bondi was twice nominated for film awards. She won an Emmy for her television appearance on *The Waltons*, playing a grandmother. After she won, she thanked her peers for honoring her while she was still alive! Beulah Bondi's career lasted forty-five years, and ironically, she never married or had a child in her private life. Her "kids" are the remarkable motion pictures we remember her for.

Beulah Bondi/Back To Bataan *(trailer)*

Thelma Ritter (1905-1969)

Thelma Ritter was a Tony award-winning actress that excelled in motion pictures. Usually playing wisecracking house servants to perfection, Ritter was nominated for an Oscar an unprecedented six times over a twelve-year period (she is tied with Deborah Kerr for female with the most nominations without a win). She was so good at off-the-cuff comedy that she co-hosted the 1954 Academy Awards show with Bob Hope. In 1957, she won her Tony for the Broadway role in *New Girl in Town.* She was a standout in her movies, including films in which she didn't even receive screen credit—*Miracle on 34th Street* and *A Letter to Three Wives.* Her characterizations were the inspiration to television's *Hazel.* She appeared as the hired help in *All about Eve* (the most nominated film in Academy history), *Rear Window*, *With a Song in My Heart*, *The Mating Season*, *Pillow Talk*, and *Boeing Boeing.* She co-starred in Arthur Miller's *The Misfits,* the final film of Clark Gable and Marilyn Monroe.

Ritter also made a number of historical dramas, including *Titanic*, featured as the very real "Unsinkable" Molly Brown (the actress who

Thelma Ritter/Mating Season *(trailer)*

survives the ordeal); *How the West Was Won*, playing a woman traveling in an 1850 wagon train from St. Louis to California; and *The Birdman of Alcatraz*, co-starring as the real-life mother of Robert Stroud, sentenced to prison for murdering a guard.

Stroud began his stretch in 1909, receiving the death penalty. President Woodrow Wilson commuted his sentence in 1920. Stroud wrote two books while incarcerated including one on bird remedies and another on

Birdman Of Alcatraz *(trailer)*

the history of the U.S. penal system. Despite his literary work, he was routinely denied parole and died in prison the day before John Kennedy was assassinated in 1963. Stroud spent fifty-four years behind bars, forty-two in solitary confinement.

Robert Stroud *(mugshot)*

I applaud the female character actors of the studio era that made a difference in tinsel town and their concerted efforts to bring history and literature to the screen.

CHAPTER THIRTEEN

FROM FOIL TO SLEUTH
Basil Rathbone (1892-1967)

THE VICTORIAN AGE CULMINATED FROM CENTURIES of kings, queens, barons, and earls establishing all that is proper in jolly old England. Royalty dictated society's behavior, and this included manner of speech, wardrobe, and etiquette. The rest of the world marveled at the British way of doing things. And, the upper crust of this great nation looked down its collective nose at the idea of imitation. When Queen Victoria died in 1901, no one could realize that the twentieth century was about to hand England a rude awakening. Yet, the Great War, the abdication of King Edward VIII in 1936 (to marry a divorced socialite), the surrender and evacuation of Dunkirk by the British Allies, the German *blitz* of 1940, the British Invasion led by The Beatles and others in rock and roll, and the very real soap opera in the marriage of Prince Charles and

Queen Victoria *(portrait)*

British Soldiers Preparing For War
(after German blitz)

Princess Diana Spencer (culminating in her untimely death) had all dealt this once proud country a crushing blow to its collective ego.

Through it all, Hollywood has had a love affair with the idea of the Victorian Age. Among the best examples

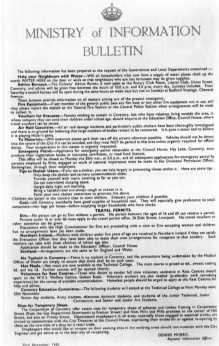

Ministry Of Information Bulletin
(during WW II)

William Shakespeare (portrait)

of this tryst was the career of Basil Rathbone. Born at the tail end of the Queen's reign, Rathbone was actually South African. However, he was a proper English gentleman that excelled in period films, usually as the suave (if cold-hearted) villain. His career began with appearing in a great number of Shakespeare's works on stage, including ***The Taming of the Shrew***, ***As You Like It***, ***A Midsummer Night's Dream***, *and* ***The Tempest.*** He toured the U.S. in the 1920s with a company and caught the attention of

Hollywood at the end of the silent era.

His first "talkie" was in ***The Bishop Murder Case***, portraying Detective Philo Vance, who was a forerunner to Nick Charles of the ***Thin Man*** series. Ironically, when Rathbone was finally later cast as a hero, he would forever be known as the quintessential detective. However, that was almost a decade away.

Captain Blood *(trailer)*

The thirties painted Basil Rathbone in period pieces that enabled him to show off his definitive skill as a swordsman. Rathbone was so precise in his ability that he would (in some cases) choreograph dueling scenes. In fencing, he was "Fred Astaire" with a foil. Since he was the villain in most of these pictures, he would almost always lose the fight but not before putting on an honorable display. His confrontations included duels with Errol Flynn in ***Captain Blood*** and ***The Adventures of Robin Hood*** (playing effec-

Tower Of London *(fencing demonstration)*

tively the evil Sir Guy of Gisbourne), Leslie Howard in ***Romeo And Juliet*** (as Tybalt), and Tyrone Power in ***The Mark of Zorro***. He also had memorable swordfights in ***The Tower of London*** and with Danny Kaye in ***The Court Jester***.

Rathbone was quite comfortable in period movies and, particularly, films that showcased his Victorian upbringing. ***David Copperfield***, ***A Tale of Two Cities***, and ***The Adventures of Marco Polo*** were exciting challenges for this gifted actor. He appeared in two exceptional films in 1939, **The Dawn Patrol** (again with Errol Flynn) and the third installment of the Mary Shelley horror classic, **The Son of Frankenstein**. In the latter film, he plays the son of the monster's creator, Baron Wolf Frankenstein. Essentially, the co-star of the film with Boris Karloff (as the creature) and Bela Lugosi, Rathbone must once again face down the demons of his family and a townsfolk weary of the Frankenstein curse. His drive as an actor made him an obvious successor to the original doctor played by Colin Clive, who had died prematurely two years before.

Baron Frankenstein
(the real one!)

It was in this eventful year that he took on a role that would forever typecast the rest of his career. Sir Arthur Conan Doyle was a noted physician and author who created the character Sherlock Holmes. Here was a sleuth honed in the Victorian age that searched for the ultimate motivations for crimes as passionately as his tracking of criminals. His most convenient foe was the ardent Professor Moriarty, every bit as brilliant as he was evil. His companions against crime were the blustery Dr.

Sir Arthur Conan Doyle

Sherlock Holmes *(drawing)*

Watson and the usually inept Inspector Lestrade of Scotland Yard. Sherlock Holmes has provided more fodder for Hollywood than any series in celluloid history, including Tarzan, Lassie, and James Bond. Many actors had their chance to play Holmes over the last seventy years, including John Barrymore, Reginald Owen, Raymond Massey, and Christopher Lee. But it was Basil Rathbone who ultimately stamped his signature as the great detective, beginning with *The Hound of the Baskervilles*.

Professor Moriarty *(drawing)*

Basil Rathbone and Nigel Bruce (as Dr. Watson) would portray the driven sleuth and his friend fourteen times on film and countless more on radio. Here was an actor that captured the essence of an age that Brits could be proud of. His forensic ability and hunches ("Elementary, my dear Watson") are legendary in Doyle's writings and Rathbone's performance. Most of the films that were produced from 20th Century Fox and Universal Studios were "B" movies, but immensely popular with the theater-going crowd. And the films differed from the usual mystery-genre of "whodunit" that was typical of Agatha Christie's books (for example). Audiences frequently knew who the villain was but marveled at Holmes' conclusive ability to trap a criminal.

The relationship scenario of Holmes and Watson was often imitated in films that replicated England of the nineteenth century. For example, *Around The World In 80 Days* offered a precise Phileas Fogg and company at a gentleman's club in London. David Niven and Robert Morley (among others) were quite similar in

Sherlock Holmes Four-Act Play *(circa 1900 lithograph)*

Basil Rathbone and Nigel Bruce/
Dressed To Kill *(trailer)*

approach as Fogg looks forward to the future, while his compatriots cling to the past with regards to aspects of time and travel. The King's English is at the heart of ***My Fair Lady***. Rex Harrison as Professor Henry Higgins and Audrey Hepburn's Eliza Doolittle certainly remakes ***Pygmalion*** as its plot, but his friendship with houseguest, Colonel Pickering (played by Wilfred Hyde White) is pure Holmes and Watson. Higgins is the master of linguistics while Pickering marvels at his proper use of language. They bask in their supposed glory of transforming a flower girl into a woman of society. The motion picture ***Sleuth*** is homage to the writings of Arthur Conan Doyle, which examines the idea of motivation in crime. The film is essentially a two-man show that stars Laurence Olivier and Michael Caine.

Unfortunately, Universal made the decision to shift Sherlock Holmes' life to days surrounding World War II, making the Nazis convenient enemies for the master sleuth. Rathbone and Bruce took it in stride, providing quaint portrayals at a time when the world was changing. When Nigel Bruce died in 1953, Rathbone lost his desire to play the great detective.

Basil Rathbone lived long enough to see his England fall from grace as a super-power. However, his roles offer a glimpse of its beloved and glorious past. He can be credited for keeping the British Empire intact through his magnificent portrayals.

Basil Rathbone/Tovarich *(trailer)*

AFTERWORD

TERMS ARE USED IN THIS BOOK that were relevant to the times. The word "Negro" is the appropriate reference of African Americans of the thirties and the forties. For example, I use it in the same way that blacks of the day defined hymns in church (the Negro Spiritual). The application of "redskin" to describe Indians is a common negative slur in Westerns of the period by protagonists and villains alike in movies and novels. I don't necessarily endorse the use of either terminology in society or in film. However, they hold historical value and impact. As CNN's Larry King once wrote, "Let's not become so worried about not offending anybody that we lose the ability to distinguish between respect and paranoia..."

"Step In The Right Direction"
(editorial cartoon)

My goal was to capture the context of the life and times of a recent era long gone and almost forgotten. Hollywood has provided us all with a visual scrapbook of the past. I am humbled to have scratched the surface with a modest contribution, recounting portions of the rich history we all share as a nation.

Appendix
DISCLAIMERS

Wikipedia & Freebase

Some text facts and photos were found on wikipedia.org and free-base.com (the world's database).

Wikipedia content is licensed under the GNU Free Documentation License (GFDL) which is a copyleft license for free documentation, designed by the Free Software Foundation (FSF) for the GNU Project. It is similar to the GNU General Public License, giving readers the rights to copy, redistribute, and modify a work and requires all copies and derivatives to be available under the same license. Copies may also be sold commercially, but, if produced in larger quantities (greater than one hundred), the original document or source code must be made available to the work's recipient.

Freebase Content is "freely licensed" under GFDL or Creative Commons Attribution (BY) which allows one to share and remix (create derivative works), even for commercial use, so long as attribution is given.

Photos found on the above Websites were confirmed in the Public Domain (PD-US). Specific Reasons can be found here in the Appendix.

Full articles on chapter subjects and themes might be found on wikipedia.org

Oscars/Academy Awards

"Academy Awards" and "Oscar" are registered trademarks and service marks of the Academy of Motion Picture Arts & Sciences (A.M.P.A.S.). The copyrighted Award of Merit ("Oscar") statuette is identified as copr. A.M.P.A.S. In addition the "Oscar" statuette and depictions thereof are trade names of A.M.P.A.S.

Movie Trailers

HTTP://WWW.CREATIVECLEARANCE.COM/GUIDELINES.HTML#D2:

Most trailers prior to 1976 were created as new works, which contained new material (such as "Coming Soon," etc.) as well as scenes from the films they were advertising. Trailers did not contain copyright notices nor were they registered in the Copyright Office or the Library of Congress. Consequently, the new material at the very least went into the Public Domain. Many of these trailers also contained material that appeared to be from the movie but was actually shot directly for the trailer. That material, since it did not contain a copyright notice, would also fall into the Public Domain.

The major argument has been that the scenes from the film itself were protected by the copyright on the complete film. However, one could argue that once you cut a clip from a film, it is a separate entity, and without a complete and separate copyright and notice, it, too, becomes Public Domain by its publication. In any event, industry custom and practice has been to use trailers prior to 1972 based on the above information.

Furthermore, trailers prior to 1960 offer an additional incentive since, under SAG rules, theatrical feature films prior to 1960 do not require residuals to be paid to actors, writers, and directors when the entire film is broadcast. Consequently, writers and directors in clips and trailers do not have to be paid and actors do not have to be cleared or paid as long as the trailer clearly identifies the film on screen over the clip as it is played or it is identified verbally. This information is not contained in the SAG Code Book but can be obtained from a SAG representative via a telephone call.

Trailers for movies released before 1964 are in the Public Domain because they were never separately copyrighted. The law at the time granted the owner twenty-eight years to file a copyright registration. Clearly, time has run out to register this material. Some might argue that, since the trailers frequently contain the same material that's in the movie and the movie is presumably copyrighted, this would cover the trailer as well. However, the trailer is published (run in a theater) before the movie itself is published. Thus, the trailer requires a separate copyright, and the scenes contained in the trailer are in Public Domain. Note that all trailers, regardless of year, until the late 80s, are o.k. to use if they contain no copyright notice. This does occur (although infrequently).

National Archives and Records Administration, Library of Congress, U.S. Senate, & Presidential Libraries

Photos and pictures from National Archives and Records Adminsitration were given specific permission for use in this book. They have been confirmed use unrestricted.

Photographs and pictures from the Library of Congress Prints and Photographs Division had no known copyright restrictions on publication. In some cases copyright had expired or was given specific permission for use as a gift of the photographer, artist, or owner of the material. Some photos may require the condition that it not be altered or cropped.

The U.S. Senate Commission on Art and the U.S. Senate Historical Office gave specific permission for photographs and pictures printed in this book.

The Presidential Libraries of Franklin D. Roosevelt, John F. Kennedy, Lyndon B. Johnson, Richard M. Nixon, and Ronald Reagan gave specific permission for photographs and pictures obtained for use in this book.

Miscellanious and Specific Use Conditions
(ie., Wikipedia & Freebase Images)

U.S. Government images may enter the Public Domain under the terms of Title 17, Chapter 1, Section 105 of the U. S. Code.

Pre-1923 photographs may enter the Public Domain because of copyright expiration.

Motion picture quotes are used in various chapters. The motion pictures are cited before or after each quote.

CHAPTER 1

Richard the Lion-Hearted drawing - François Guizot (1787-1874), *The History of France from the Earliest Times to the Year 1789*, London: S. Low, Marston, Searle & Rivington, 1883, p. 419. Author - Alphonse Marie de Neuville. A mere photograph of an out-of-copyright two-dimensional work may not be protected under American copyright law and is in Public Domain.

CHAPTER 2

Frank Capra photograph - Date: 1943. This image is a work of a U.S. Army soldier or employee, taken or made during the course of the person's official duties. As a work of the U.S. Federal Government, the image is in the Public Domain (PD) under the terms of Title 17, Chapter 1, Section 105 of the U.S. Code.

Lionel Barrymore/Armed Forces Radio Show photograph - Circa 1947. This image is a work of a U.S. Military or Department of Defense employee, taken or made during the course of an employee's official duties. As a work of the U.S. Federal Government, the image is in the Public Domain (PD) under the terms of Title 17, Chapter 1, Section 105 of the U.S. Code.

CHAPTER 3

Aimee Semple McPherson/"Arrested For Speeding" photograph - Foursquare Heritage Archives, Los Angeles, California. 1925 photo at Angelus Temple (permission personally granted for use in this book)

Arthur Miller photograph - U.S. Department of State employee took the photo during the course of his or her duties. Public Domain (PD-U.S. Gov-State Dept.) under the terms of Title 17, Chapter 1, Section 105 of the U.S. Code.

Salem Witch Trial drawing - *Pioneers in the Settlement of America* by William A. Crafts. Vol. I Boston: Samuel Walker & Company, 1876. A mere photograph of an out-of-copyright two-dimensional work may not be protected under American copyright law and is in Public Domain (PD).

Arthur Kennedy Tombstone photograph - Ivan Smith (Canning, Nova Scotia) photo taken on July 10, 2003; Mr. Smith has personally given permission to use the photo in this book.

B-17 Bomber photograph - This image is a work of a U.S. Air Force airman or employee, taken or made during the course of the person's official duties. As a work of the U.S. Federal Government, the image or file is in the Public Domain (PD) under the terms of Title 17, Chapter 1, Section 105 of the U.S. Code.

CHAPTER 4

Adam Helmer Gravesite photograph - Catherine Nonenmacher photo taken on October 5, 2004. The copyright holder of this work released it into the Public Domain (PD). This applies worldwide.

Morgan Earp photograph - Probably taken by C.S. Fly, 1881. Copyright has expired.

Ayn Rand text - Appears originally from a pamphlet for the Motion Picture Alliance for the Preservation of American Ideals

CHAPTER 5

Alvin York photograph - Pfc. F.C. Phillips photograph, February 7, 1919. This image is a work of a U.S. military or Department of Defense employee, taken or made during the course of an employee's official duties. As a work of the U.S. Federal Government, the image is in the Public Domain (PD) under the terms of Title 17, Chapter 1, Section 105 of the U.S. Code.

James Stewart photograph - Taken by U.S. Air Force airmen or employee. As a work of the U. S. Federal Government, the image is in the Public Domain (PD) under the terms of Title 17, Chapter 1, Section 105 of the U.S. Code.

Edison Movie Studios photograph - circa 1907-1918. Copyright has expired.

Old Man Clanton photograph - Taken in the mid-1800s. No known copyright restriction.

CHAPTER 6

Hattie McDaniel photograph - Myra Wysinger photo from album collection. This image has been (or is hereby) released into the Public Domain (PD). This applies worldwide and grants anyone the right to use this work for any purpose, without any conditions.

Sullivan Brothers photograph - U. S. Naval Historical Center. This image is a work of a U.S. military or Department of Defense employee, taken or made during the course of an employee's official duties. As a work of the U.S. Federal Government, the image is in the Public Domain (PD) under the terms of Title 17, Chapter 1, Section 105 of the U.S. Code.

No Foreign Entanglements photograph - Frame from *Prelude to War* documentary film, part of the *Why We Fight* series. This work is in the Public Doman in the U. S. (PD-U.S. Gov) under the terms of Title 17, Chapter 1, Section 105 of the U.S. Code.

Hunchback of Notre Dame drawing - Victor Hugo, *Oeuvres Illustrées de Victor Hugo*. Paris: J. Hetzel, 1853. A mere photograph of an out-of-copyright two-dimensional work may not be protected under American copyright law and is in Public Domain (PD).

Theodore Roosevelt Gravesite photograph - Laurie Pacheco photo. This photograph belongs to the author and its copyrighted use is solely for this book or author-related books.

CHAPTER 7

Robert Ford photograph - An unknown author (taken between 1882 and 1892). No known copyright restriction.

Jesse James dime novel photograph - A mere photograph of an out-of-copyright two-dimensional work may not be protected under American copyright law and is in Public Domain (PD).

Jules Verne dime novel photograph - scanned Historiograf 1884. A mere photograph of an out-of-copyright two-dimensional work may not be protected under American copyright law and is in Public Domain (PD).

Aaron and The Golden Calf painting - Nicolas Poussin. A mere photograph of an out-of-copyright two-dimensional work may not be protected under American copyright law and is in Public Domain (PD).

Stagecoach drawing - "The Stage," illustration of "A Peep at Washoe" by J. Ross Browne, January 1861. *Harper's Monthly Magazine*, Vol. XXII, p. 148, Harper Brothers, New York. A mere photograph of an out-of-copyright two-dimensional work may not be protected under American copyright law and is in the Public Domain (PD).

Ann Frank House photograph - Laurie Pacheco photo. This photograph belongs to the author and its copyrighted use is solely for this book or author-related books.

Jules Verne autograph - date unknown. A mere photograph of an out-of-copyright two-dimensional work may not be protected under American copyright law and is in the Public Domain (PD).

CHAPTER 8

War of the Worlds drawing - Alien tripod from 1906 French edition of H.G. Wells' *War of the Worlds*. Illustration by Alvim Corréa. A mere photograph of an out-of-copyright two-dimensional work may not be protected under American copyright law and is in the Public Domain (PD).

Guadalcanal Campaign photograph - John L. Zimmerman (1949). This image is a work of a sailor or employee of the U.S. Navy, taken or made during the course of the person's official duties. As a work of the U.S. Federal Government, the image is in the Public Domain (PD) under the terms of Title 17, Chapter 1, Section 105 of the U. S. Code.

CHAPTER 9

Grand Tetons photograph - Jon Sullivan has released this photo into the Public Domain (PD) for any and all use worldwide. Courtesy of pdphoto.org.

D.W. Griffith postage stamp photograph - Postage stamp owned by Swollib at Wikipedia. This work is in the Public Domain (PD) in the United States because it is a work of U.S. Federal Government under the terms of Title 17, Chapter 1, Section 105 of the the U.S. Code.

Walter Reed photograph - Photograph about 1890. This image is in the Public Domain (PD) because its copyright has expired.

King Lear page photograph - Title page of the first edition of *King Lear* by William Shakespeare (1608). A mere photograph of an out-of-copyright two-dimensional work may not be protected under American copyright law and is in the Public Domain (PD).

Collie drawing - Pearson Scott Foresman has released this picture into the Public Domain (PD) for any and all use worldwide.

Teton Range map - Grand Teton by the National Park Service. This work is in the Public Domain (PD) in the U.S. because it is a work of the United States Federal Government under the terms of Title 17, Chapter 1, Section 105 of the U.S. Code.

Thaddeus Stevens portrait - Carl Schurz, *Reminiscences*, Volume Three, McClure Publishing Co., 1907, facing p. 214. This media file is in the Public Domain (PD) in the U.S. This applies to U.S. works where the copyright has expired.

CHAPTER 10

Three Musketeers drawing - *The Three Musketeers* by Alexandre Dumas, 1894. Author - Maurice Leloir. Faithful reproductions of two-dimensional works of art are Public Domain (PD).

Pancho Villa Expedition photograph - C. Tucker Beckett, 1916. This photo by flashlight powder. Image is a work of a U. S. military or Department of Defense employee, taken or made during the course of an employee's official duties. As a work of the U.S. federal government, the image is in the Public Domain (PD) under the terms of Title 17, Chapter 1, Section 105 of the U.S. Code.

Texas Theatre photograph - Michael Dorash photo of Oak Hill, Texas theatre, June 2008. The copyright holder of this work, hereby releases it into the Public Domain. This applies worldwide.

Lee Harvey Oswald photographs - Warren Commission Report Vol. 26 p. 445 bears no copyright notice.

CHAPTER 11

Colin Powell photograph - Author unknown. Image is a work of a U.S. Department of State employee taken during the course of his or her duties. This photo is in the Public Domain (PD-U.S. Gov-State Department) under the terms of Title 17, Chapter 1, Section 105 of the U.S. Code.

CHAPTER 12

Betsy Ross House photograph - Avishai Teicher photo. This image has been released into the Public Domain (PD) by its author, for any purpose, without any conditions.

Robert Stroud photographs - Mug shot, October 1951. Image is a work of a U.S. Department of Justice employee, taken or made during the course of an employee's official duties. As a work of the U.S. Federal Government, the image is in the Public Domain (PD) under the terms of Title 17, Chapter 1, Section 105 of the U.S. Code.

CHAPTER 13

Fencing Demonstration photograph - Laurie Pacheco photo. This photograph belongs to the author and its copyrighted use is solely for this book or author-related books.

Sherlock Holmes drawing - Sidney Paget, 1904. A mere photograph of an out-of-copyright two-dimensional work may not be protected under American copyright law and is in the Public Domain (PD).

Professor Moriarty drawing - Sidney Paget. A mere photograph of an out-of-copyright two-dimensional work may not be protected under American copyright law and is in the Public Domain (PD).

Eddie Anderson

THE MAN JACK BENNY DISCOVERED... OR VICE VERSA

"Rochester"

ABOUT THE AUTHOR

MANNY PACHECO IS A RADIO AND TELEVISION PERSONALITY from Orange County, California. His career has spanned over three decades. He was a host of the Daytime Emmy-nominated, *In Studio* on **KCOP 13**. He has also appeared on **NBC's *Santa Barbara***, and moderated many public television pledge drives (**KCET** in Los Angeles). He also had a principle role in the documentary, ***Karaoke Fever***, which was featured at the **L.A. Film Festival** in 2001.

Manny currently works in voice-over and commercial acting, and his clients have included FORD, GTE, ARCO, MILLER LITE, and most recently, HONDA. Since 1980, he has been a broadcaster, newscaster and traffic reporter for stations in Los Angeles his entire career.

A 27-year member of the Screen Actor's Guild and a member of the American Television and Radio Artists, Manny recently wrote an article about his experiences at ***The 2008 Screen Actors Guild Awards*** that appeared on a blog at L.A. Radio.com and Karaoke Scene Magazine in Southern California. Many of his articles have appeared in Karaoke Scene Magazine.

An L.A.-native, Manny received his undergraduate degree at UCLA in Bachelor of Arts, Political Science Major. He is married to Laurie and they currently live in Cypress.